What readers are sa
The Art of the Almost

The Art of the Almost Said is one of the best books on poetry I have ever read. Robert Hudson writes as both a writer of poetry and a reader of it, the latter partly in his role as a poetry editor. This is a how-to-do-it book of the highest order. Practical tips abound, including sections at the end of chapters with exercises and suggestions for readings. In summary, this book has something for everyone—for readers and teachers of poetry as much as for poets.

—Leland Ryken, author and scholar

Far and away the best book I've ever read on the art and the commerce of poetry. The lyrical and sometimes wrenching insights of poet/author Robert Hudson, its encouraging and practical suggestions and exercises, and the acknowledgment of the nobility and ennobling qualities of poetry make it a treasure.

—Latayne C. Scott, award-winning author, *A Conspiracy of Breath* and *Passion, Power, Proxy, Release*

When I was starting out in poetry, I would have been so excited to find this book that I would have taken it straight to the cash register and then straight home to read it straight through. Robert Hudson is a skilled fellow practitioner, a naysayer to the naysayers, a contrarian's contrarian, and a master encourager. This is the most practical of books because it does not demystify its subject. Instead it inspires you to sit down to write, and to live a life in poetry. First rate.

—Brian G. Phipps, poet, *Before the Burning Bush*

Robert Hudson has written the ideal introduction for the poetry novice. It is eminently approachable, wise, and a bit whimsical, yet it honors the mystery at the heart of a really good poem. Hudson explores how a poet works, how a poem is put together, and how one might get one's own poetic work into print. If you've ever found yourself moved by a poem but didn't exactly understand why, or if you've ever wanted to try your hand at writing one for yourself, you'll find what you are looking for in this delightful venture into the world of poetry.

—Terry Glaspey, award-winning author, *75 Masterpieces Every Christian Should Know*

Robert Hudson has given us a walkabout through the veldts, mountains, deserts, cities and forests of his more than fifty years in the poetry trade. This is a delightful, informed, and serendipitous volume that barely conceals Hudson's not-so-hidden agenda, which borrows from Ezra Pound's stated intent 100 years ago to "resuscitate the dead art." Hudson is a gentle general leading the charge to recruit and train legions of new poets and poetry lovers from every walk of life. This book inspires, cajoles and teases its readers to express themselves creatively.

—Bruce Edward Walker, host, the Acton Institute for the Study of Religion's Upstream culture podcast

The Art of the

almost said

Also by Robert Hudson

Kiss the Earth When You Pray: The Father Zosima Poems
The Monk's Record Player: Thomas Merton, Bob Dylan, and the Perilous Summer of 1966
Four Birds of Noah's Ark: A Prayer Book from the Time of Shakespeare (by Thomas Dekker, edited with an introduction by Robert Hudson)
The Christian Writer's Manual of Style, 4th Edition
Companions for the Soul (Robert Hudson and Shelley Townsend-Hudson)
Beyond Belief: What the Martyrs Said to God (Duane W. H. Arnold and Robert Hudson)

Chapbooks:

Making a Poetry Chapbook
Listen: Twenty-One Nazms on Prayer
Rondels for After: Translations of Poems by Tristan Corbière
Bugs: A Haiku Anthology
Very Like a Whale
Authors and Their Pets
Max among the Trees
Proof or Consequences

The Art of the almost said

A Christian Writer's Guide to Writing Poetry

Robert Hudson

A Nuts 'n Bolts Book

Bold Vision Books
PO Box 2011
Friendswood, Texas 77549

The Art of the Almost Said

Cover design by Maddie Scott
Interior design by *k*ae Creative Solutions

Nuts 'n Bolts is an imprint of Bold Vision Books
Published by Bold Vision Books, PO Box 2011, Friendswood, Texas 77549
www.boldvisionbooks.com Email: boldvisionbooks@gmail.com

Published in association with the literary agency of Credo Communications, LLC, Grand Rapids, MI 49525; www.credocommunications.net.

Printed in the United States of America

To the awesome people of *WorkingPOET* (2000–2004):
Laura Blost, Sue Johnson, Deborah Leiter,
Brian Phipps, and Angela Scheff—
and to working poets
everywhere

And to
the memory of
Uncle John Anderson, my jo

Contents

Poetry is the almost said.

~Juan Ramón Jiménez[1]

Foreword

Eric L. Motley

Sing them over again to me,
Wonderful words of life,
Let me more of their beauty see,
Wonderful words of life;
Words of life and beauty
Teach me faith and duty.

... Beautiful words, wonderful words,
Wonderful words of life;
Beautiful words, wonderful words,
Wonderful words of life.

—poet P. P. Bliss, 1874

At an early age, I came to discover the wonderment of words. A college mentor many years later even once suggested that they are a revelation of our selfhood, a window through which others view our souls. Words have such power. And all these years later I remain utterly fascinated with their simple brilliance and even how they are strung together to reach certain ends. How they glisten on a page—how they carry with them meaning and significance, aspirations and hopes, and even the promise of the totally unknown. Indeed "wonderful words of life."

My first introduction to poetry was when I was three or four years old. Recitation was very much a part of my upbringing, and every Christmas and Easter demanded my learning a little poem or ditty and reciting it before the entire church congregation at the holiday pageant. How wonderfully exciting to have an entire audience of hundreds of people listening, but the real excitement came in the preparation—learning the words, fashioning the pronunciation of words from mind to mouth, and confidently owning them and speaking them out loud. At the age of eight, poetry and recitation had become so much a part of my life that it became a daily ritual for me to stand and recite an entire poem or a stanza at the dinner table.

In my mind, memory was majestic. My grandmother would always encourage me to commit verse to memory because I would eventually find in those ideas a sure refuge that I could always summon to heart and mind in all seasons of life. So since those early years I have had a love affair with words, with language, and in particular a love affair with poetry. In those early years, I came to know William Wordsworth, Gerard Manley Hopkins, Shakespeare, Shelley, Keats, Langston Hughes, Robert Frost, Henry Wadsworth Longfellow, and Gwendolyn Brooks, just to name a few. I started to carry poems in my pocket and in my wallet, and often when I am sitting by myself in an airport, or waiting in line, or on a long conference call, or just needing a spiritual distraction, I take out a poem and read it to myself and sometimes even to others. I have done it so often that now friends and colleagues ask me to pull a poem from my pocket to read.

About fifteen years ago I became more serious about poetry and set out more deliberately and intentionally to start reading as many living poets as possible, to meet them, and to develop meaningful relationships with them. Richard Wilbur, Maya Angelou, Wendell Berry, Elizabeth Alexander, Dana Gioia, Natasha Trethewey have all helped me to see more clearly, to listen more nearly, to honor words more dearly. And in unintended ways they have also helped to quicken my own desire to unashamedly write more and to share my own verse with friends and fellow poets, although I still see myself as a poet manqué. But I am very much in the sport of it and still learning and growing and discovering what I call the "art and science" of writing verse. It is not the writing, the first draft or the second draft, but it is the editing—the rewriting and rewriting—where the most labor is expended.

Poet Robert Hudson knows the intricacies—the "art and science" of poetry. He knows very well where the most labor is expended. He knows poetry because first and foremost he is a poet. He is daring and innovative in form, meter, and imagery. His verse captures his wide-ranging emotional and intellectual awareness. He started out as a teacher but soon abandoned the classroom to become a book editor. But at the very heart of his being he remains a teacher, and reading this book is like sitting in a classroom as someone with experience in all aspects of writing and publishing explains the processes of both very carefully. So be sure to take notes. Hudson ranges from the hard-to-define aspects of writing poems to the nuts-and-bolts of actually getting your work out there in front of readers. In this regard, this book is a guide to how to be a poet who not only writes well but is worthy of being read by others.

Hudson has a passion for encouraging young people. He organized the internship program for Zondervan for more than thirty years, working with seventy or eighty young people, some of whom have gone on to become leaders in the publishing world. Our legacy does not live only in our achievements but in the people we have cared for and encouraged along the way.

To a very large degree, Hudson's conviction is that poetry characteristically comes out of faith. Faith is not lost in words; rather, words manifest faith. And though it's not stated, the spirit of Madeleine L'Engle is found in these pages—in the idea that you should strive to be a writer first, and your Christianity will be obvious. But to insert your faith in some artificial way is the definition of insincerity.

I adamantly believe that poetry is needed now, perhaps, more than any other time. In his 2013 Ted Talk, poet and literary critic Stephen Burt affirmed, "Poetry isn't one thing that serves one purpose any more than music or computer programming serve one purpose. The Greek word *poem*, it just means 'a made thing,' and poetry is a set of techniques, ways of making patterns that put emotions into words. The more techniques you know, the more things you can make, and the more patterns you can recognize in things you might already like or love."

In our culture that is dominated by angry, dissonant voices, we must all strive to make more patterns, to render our emotions in more carefully chosen words, and to discover and rediscover beauty and what we like and love. As Hudson says, "If everyone who wrote just one poem this year were to buy just one book of poetry by a living poet … we could start a literary revolution." We could also begin it by reading and encouraging others to read *The Art of the Almost Said.*

I wish I had read it when I was younger. It might have saved me a lot of trial and error.

—Eric L. Motley, Executive Vice President and Corporate Secretary, The Aspen Institute

A Note to the Reader

This book is *not* for the poetry professional, nor is it written *by* a poetry professional. It's for the struggling poet, the wanting-to-get-better poet, the hoping-to-publish-someday poet.

My primary qualification is that I'm a struggling poet myself and have been for more than fifty years. Although I've been an avid poetry reader and writer since grade school ... although I studied it formally in college and graduate school and spent a brief, inglorious stint as a poetry editor for a literary journal ... although I ran a small, now-defunct poetry website, wrote a poetry blog, and with my wife still own a cheerfully money-losing chapbook press that publishes poetry ... and although my poems get published from time to time—despite that, I'm a novice. And a proud one. What monk and poet Thomas Merton said of the spiritual life is as true of poetry: "Let us be convinced of the fact that we will never be anything else but beginners, all our life!"[1]

But I also write this book from the perspective of a manuscript editor of more than three decades, one who has worked with all kinds of writers, including poets. My trade has been to encourage authors to ratchet up their craft a couple of notches. The musings in these pages grew out of my own experience as a writing coach, a book doctor, a teacher of literature, a champion of written style, and a stringer together of words.

Each section of this book presents one small step in the practice of writing poems:

- Part One introduces the basics: reading, silence, process, and creativity.
- Part Two assembles the elements that make up a poem, like form and voice, and explores a few

mysterious places where inspiration might be found; from a walk in the woods to the inner reaches of the unconscious mind.
- Part Three dissects some common obstacles—like writer's block and depression—that keep good poems from happening.
- Part Four discusses readership, explains the how-tos of submitting poems to magazines, and suggests ways to reach your ideal reader—whether through publication or creative alternatives.

Many chapters end with practical exercises as well as suggested readings, which include general resources and books by both classic and contemporary poets.

Throughout, my method is to come at poetry from odd angles, tell quirky anecdotes, indulge in gossip about the lives of poets, and provide off-the-wall quotations—all of which, sooner or later, come 'round to making serious connections in the hope of shaking loose some creativity and provoking fresh ideas. That method, as one friend said, is like "a long, slow wind-up for a fast pitch."

My hope is that these reflections on the craft of poetry will help you find the poems you were meant to write.

The poems are out there. Trust them.

The rest is up to you.

—Robert Hudson

The Art of the

almost said

On our earth, before writing was invented, before the printing press was invented, poetry flourished. That is why we know that poetry is like bread; it should be shared by all, by scholars and by peasants, by all our vast, incredible, extraordinary family of humanity.

—Pablo Neruda (1904–1973)[1]

1

The Working Poet

A great uncle on my mother's side was an engineer, a gardener, a poet, and the possessor of one of the sunshiniest smiles on earth. Uncle John's short, neatly rhyming poems—politely called "verse"—were about flowers, the seasons of the year, and the weather, and he published them in small gardening magazines in the 1950s and '60s.

One year, he spent Easter weekend at our house. I was a sullen teenager at the time, writing dark poetry and engrossed in Dylan Thomas and Charles Baudelaire. But Uncle John and I shared a bond, an unspoken contract that those who love poetry stick together.

As often happened, someone asked him to recite at the dinner table. Slowly he extracted a sheaf of papers from the inner pocket of his coat, selected a poem, and rose from his chair in what I can only describe as a rhetorical sort of way.

I don't remember what he read, one of his flower poems most likely, but when he was done, my grandfather, Uncle John's brother, to forestall a second recitation, bellowed, "Oh, John, sit down! That's just old doggerel and you know it!"

Without missing a beat, Uncle John turned in my direction and, flashing one of his solar smiles, said, "Yes, but us dogs don't mind, do we, Bob?"

Us Dogs

As a teenager, I was more than engrossed in Dylan Thomas; I wanted to *be* Dylan Thomas. Now, in my sixties, I realize I could do worse than to be Uncle John.

You see, to be Dylan Thomas, you give up a lot, not the least of which is losing your life to alcohol before you're forty. (Baudelaire managed to make it to forty-six.) You sacrifice health, peace of mind, any semblance of a normal life, and many of your closest relationships—all on the altar of poetry. A fair number of poets have done that in some form or other, and on rare occasions the result is brilliant poetry. Most often it's not.

Uncle John, by contrast, put in his forty hours at a nine-to-five job, came home, wrote verse, went to bed early, and always had a kind of exhilarated, restless contentment about him. He loved people, found humor in every situation, and saw the miraculous everywhere—especially his garden.

He was not a great poet, but it was not for lack of enthusiasm. He worked hard at everything he did. Before World War I, he and my grandfather were the first to attend the University of Illinois without high school diplomas. Their mother had home-schooled them at night, in secret, because their Swedish-immigrant father thought schooling was a waste of his sons' time when they could be earning a living on the Rock Island road crew.

Uncle John and his wife, Gladys, were Presbyterians, though he told me once with an impish grin that they only attended church at Easter and Christmas because they couldn't stand "being around all those hypocrites the rest of year!"

If anyone, like his brother, made fun of him, he would smile and say, "Well, they just ain't got no couth, do they, Bob?"

So, as I said, one could do worse than to be Uncle John.

Although I fall short of his kindly example, in many ways I've been more fortunate. I've never been accused of writing doggerel, for one thing. Like him, I'm not a poet for the ages, but I've published a volume of poetry, a number of poetry chapbooks, and several books of prose; my poems have appeared in respected journals, and I've even been asked—and paid good money, no less—to speak at conferences about topics I love: editing, publishing, writing, inspiration, and poetry. Uncle John would have been proud.

He was also my first introduction to a "working poet."

A Working Poet

At the symphony years ago, a man introduced himself to me by saying, "I used to teach art, but now I'm a working artist," by which he meant, I think, that he was able to devote his days to painting. His wife worked full-time. The encounter got me thinking: Is it possible to be a *working poet*? Aside from the pretension of it ("Hello, yes, I'm a working poet"), the immediate answer is ... no. It's unlikely.

Even most major poets don't earn their living by poetry alone. Most teach, some lecture, some write novels or articles to keep themselves afloat—or all of that combined. The most famous survive by selling their manuscripts to archives and collectors. Aside from those who are independently wealthy or retired, most have day jobs. Every English major knows that among the great American poets, Wallace Stevens (1879–1955) was an insurance executive, William Carlos Williams (1883–1963) was a pediatrician, and Richard Hugo (1923–1982) had a desk job at Boeing. The lucky ones, such as professors and journal editors, find work peripherally related to their writing, but even in those cases, their days are filled with work other than poems.

All of which is for the best, I think. Poetry should be a nearly monastic calling, attracting those who love it for its own sake, who are called to it, who can't *not* write it. In a country that contains tens of millions of people who haven't read a poem since high school (research indicates that more than half the population hasn't even read an entire book since their school days), as well as vast hordes who claim to hate poetry, I pity the poor soul who embarks on a career as a poet expecting money and fame.

Day jobs are not only necessary, they're useful (and I include parenting among the world's most difficult jobs). If poetry "is the spontaneous overflow of powerful feelings; [and] takes its origin from emotion recollected in tranquility,"[2] as English Romantic poet William Wordsworth (1770–1850) maintained, then one at least needs some powerful feelings and emotions to recollect, and most jobs provide a lot of fodder—as well as a healthy reality check. Human interaction and the daily grind are up there with love, death, and nature as great fertilizers for poems.

For the poet, even at the worst jobs, poetry is never far away. An old Russian proverb says, "The poet always cheats the boss." What writer hasn't been struck with a line during a staff meeting or spent an extended lunch getting on paper the skeleton of an idea? You can't help but be astounded by intriguing phrases, overheard conversations, and the daily, delectable absurdity of it all. Poetry can even make a bad job tolerable.

But there is another shade of meaning to *working poet.* The term gives those of us in corporate cubicles, at receptions desks, behind counters, in cherry pickers, working in the open air or on the loading dock, clerking, changing diapers, requisitioning, filing, chopping, digging, feeding kids, wait staffing, computing—it gives all of us working folks *permission* … the much-needed permission to write poems.

Why do we need permission? Because so many books of poetry—and books about poetry—are not only written *by* professors but *for* professors. I have nothing against the "poetry professionals," though I'm jealous of even the small scraps of recognition they garner from a largely unappreciative world. Although they often write great poetry, they can, unwittingly, make the rest of us feel as though they have a prior and superior intellectual claim. They don't mean to do it, but they are the paid experts, after all—and they have letters after their names to prove it.

Still, the more you read magazines and study new volumes of poems, the more you realize that the powerful poetry-industrial complex may not be as monolithic as you might imagine. Some of that poetry is beautiful and astonishing; but a lot of it is humdrum, oppressively intellectual, dull, navel-gazing, obscure, academic, or, most particularly, self-indulgent. And, as amateurs and beginners, we have the absolute right to call them out on it.

I suspect that much of what we perceive of as that incestuous cabal of poetry professionals is in part the creation of their own insecurities—it's a secret society that doesn't exist, even though a large number of people pretend to belong to it even as they busy themselves trying to forge their own invitation to join.

But ponder this fact for a moment: after the professionals have published their "volumes," recited from podiums, and signed your copy, the universe of poetic possibility is no more limited than it was before. "For all this," says English poet and priest Gerard Manley Hopkins (1844–1889), "nature is never spent."[3] The poems you were meant to write are still out there waiting for you to write them. The experts can't take them from you. You can learn much from the professionals while ignoring their pretensions. As Uncle John would say, "They just ain't got no couth."

Poetry is for people who have something genuine, heartfelt, interesting, or quirky to say. It should be written for people who ride the bus, work the late shift, bag the leaves, or play video games … people who send birthday cards, struggle with their weight, forget to take their meds, tuck in the kids, check Facebook, and drive the dog to the vet. Or put it this way, *unless* poetry makes sense to us ordinary folks—to us dogs—it's not poetry. It's just highbrow puzzle constructing.

Encouragement and Stretching

When I speak at conferences I usually have two goals in mind: the first is to *encourage* writers, and the second is to *stretch* them. The two go hand in hand.

Encouragement is nothing more than convincing people that, while they may not be Dylan Thomas or Charles Baudelaire, they have a perspective and a voice that belong to no one else. *You* matter, I tell them. *Your* poetry matters, even if the only people who hear it are those sitting around your dinner table at Easter. But if the impulse is strong, irresistible, then you need to write those poems. No excuses.

This book, then, is one long pep talk.

The stretching is more difficult but every bit as essential. It includes, as you'll see in the next chapter, reading more—more widely and more consistently—especially those poets who make you think, who startle you, who make you uncomfortable. It includes exposing yourself to ideas you haven't thought of, to styles, techniques, forms, genres, possibilities, philosophies, and approaches that make you feel uneasy. If the poets you read now don't unsettle you, find new ones. That will mean giving up dearly held preconceptions, and it will involve looking at yourself, your most vexatious thoughts and your hardest emotions, with a cold, unbiased eye. No more fuzzy sentimentality. No more hackneyed ideas or religious commonplaces. To see yourself—your affections and confusions, your joys and agonies—as well as the world around you with unflinching and at times painful honesty is the most valuable thing you can do as well as the most discomfiting. And it's where decent poetry starts.

So expect this book to challenge as it affirms. It's okay for Christians to learn from—and love—Muslim poets and Zen masters; rappers and poetry slammers; the gay and the straight; the daring and the dissolute; the sacred, the profane, and perhaps the even more profane. Our faith is strengthened by reading poets whose lives are different than our own. It's necessary to see the world through alien eyes because we ourselves are, in the words of Abraham, "strangers and sojourners."[4] Unless we are to some degree outcasts, it will be hard for us to write.

Some of the ideas in this book will not seem quite orthodox—that is, not "comfortable." But that's all right. To write poetry, we must become comfortable with the uncomfortable because it's God's way of saying, "Get woke!" It's what keeps us thinking and alive; it's what keeps us writing.

And anyway, us dogs don't mind.

Exercises

- When in your life were you first aware of poetry? Was it read to you as a child? Did you read it to yourself? What was your experience of poetry during your school years? Who was your first favorite poet? If you haven't read that poet in a while, do so now.
- When did you first try writing poems? Did you share them with others, and what responses did you receive? Do you still have copies of your earliest poems? If so, find them and read them over.
- *Poem assignment:* Address a poem-letter to your younger self in which you summarize what you've learned about poetry (or about life) since then. Do it, perhaps, in the form of a list. Make it honest, perhaps critical or maybe comic, but most of all, *not* sentimental.

Reading

Helpful Resources

- If the work-a-day world is grinding down your creative soul, you might find this book helpful: *The Heart Aroused: Poetry and the Preservation of the Soul in Corporate America* (2002) by English poet David Whyte (b. 1955).

- A popular underground classic on the topic of surviving as an artist in the corporate world is Gordon MacKenzie's *Orbiting the Giant Hairball: A Corporate Fool's Guide to Surviving with Grace* (1998).
- For a beautifully poetic approach to these same issues, read the small volume of reflections by Spanish writer and Nobel Prize–laureate Juan Ramón Jiménez (1881–1958): *The Complete Perfectionist: A Poetics of Work* (1997), edited by Christopher Maurer.

Classic Poets

- For profound poems on the themes of faith and work, read the translations of Rumi (1207–1273) by American poet Coleman Barks (b. 1937) in the volume *One-Handed Basket Weaving: Poems on the Theme of Work* (1993).
- Read anything you can get your hands on by Walt Whitman (1819–1892). His poetry offers a grand panorama of America. Reading Whitman is one of the best ways to loosen up the stiff poetic muscles.

Contemporary Poets

- *The Republic of Poetry* (2006) by Martín Espada (b. 1957) is an encouraging book in that many of the poems are about poetry and poets, Pablo Neruda (1904–1973) and Robert Creeley (1926–2005) among others.
- The work of American poet Thomas Lynch (b. 1948) often concerns his other calling as a mortician. His book of essays called *The Undertaking: Life Studies from the Dismal Trade* (2009) is surprisingly life-affirming.

Part One: Preparations

A poem ... must be new as foam and old as the rock.

—Ralph Waldo Emerson (1803–1882)[1]

2 Reading: The Stranger on the Bus

Long ago in a land far, far away—that is, the 1960s—you could always strike up a conversation with a stranger of the opposite sex by asking, "So, how's your poetry coming?" It was a countercultural pickup line, the equivalent of "So, you come here often?" Nine times out of ten, the baffled response would be "Great, ... but how'd you know I write poetry?"

The trick, of course, was that everyone wrote poetry back then. The equivalent question today would be "So, how's your Twitter account?"

The reason that everybody wrote poetry was that everybody read it, not always great poetry, but poetry of a kind. It was part of the culture—especially the *pop* culture. It was in the air you breathed and on the airwaves you listened to.

In 1968, for example, pop singer Donovan charted at number seven on *Billboard's* Hot 100 with his spoken-word song "Atlantis," and that same year, folk icon Joan Baez released an entire album, *Baptism: A Journey Through Our Time*, of classic English poems, some spoken and some sung. Rock star Jim Morrison published a book of poetry, as did John Lennon and Yoko Ono. Talk-show host Les Crane hit number eight on the pop charts with his reading of the prose poem *Desiderata* ("Go placidly amid the noise and haste ...") by Max Ehrmann (1872–1945). Through the efforts of Caedmon Records and their amazing recordings of Dylan Thomas (1914–1953), vinyl discs of poetry readings were available in almost every record store as well as in bookshops and libraries.

In 1969, songwriter and mood poet Rod McKuen (1933–2015), whose books were probably given as gifts more often than any in history, won a Grammy for his all-poetry record *Lonesome Cities*. For a time, his books *Stanyan Street and Other Sorrows* and *Listen to the Warm* achieved cult status. A T. S. Eliot he was not, but McKuen sold far more books—more than a million copies in 1968 alone and more than 60 million over his lifetime.

English professors in the '60s engaged students by asking whether the Beatles and Bob Dylan (b. 1941) weren't really the true poets of the age, and disconcerted parents stood up at PTA meetings to ask what the heck "Eleanor Rigby" and "Mr. Tambourine Man" were doing in the high school English curriculum. Those parents could never have imagined that Dylan would one day win the Nobel Prize for literature.

The anthology *Reflections on a Gift of a Watermelon Pickle*, published in 1967, was a ubiquitous high school text and influenced an entire generation to either love or hate poetry. It's where many students back then first encountered "In Just" by E. E. Cummings (1894–1962), "Dreams" by Langston Hughes (1902–1967), and "This Is Just to Say" (that much-parodied poem about plums) by William Carlos Williams (1883–1963). The anthology was often criticized for being too "modern," for including too many *living* poets.

Of course, you can't discuss poetry in the 1960s without mentioning Kahlil Gibran (1883–1931), the third best-selling poet of all time (after Shakespeare and Lao Tzu).[2] His book of mystical, Sufi-infused prose poems, *The Prophet*, proved fairly successful when first published in 1923, but by the mid '60s, it was selling a quarter million copies annually. You were considered a social embarrassment not to have read it.

Books of poems signaled important rites of passage. Countless students, who had been raised on *Winnie-the-Pooh*, now headed off to college with *Coney Island of the Mind* by Beat poet Lawrence Ferlinghetti (b. 1919) tucked into their army-surplus backpacks, and many women remember first reading *Ariel* by Sylvia Plath (1932–1963) and her novel *The Bell Jar* the way others remember the moon landing. In 1965, poet Dudley Randall (1914–2000) founded the Broadside Press, thereby giving a new voice to an entire generation of poets in the black community.

The publication of certain volumes marked cultural watersheds. Poetry lovers still talk about the impact of *Life Studies* by Robert Lowell (1917–1977), which won the National Book Award in 1960, as well as *Nights and Days* by James Merrill (1926–1995), which won the award in 1967. In 1968, *In the Mecca* by Pulitzer Prize–winner Gwendolyn Brooks (1917–2000) became a model for socially engaged poetry. The innovative *77 Dream Songs* by John Berryman (1914–1972) and *Live or Die* by Anne Sexton (1928–1974), which won Pulitzers in 1965 and 1967 respectively, were landmarks—seminal and still highly regarded.

It was a heady, formative time, and yet …

Our Poets

In poetry, as in life, nostalgia, if allowed to linger, starts to smell like something left too long in the vegetable drawer. Whether we're talking about the Romantic poets of the nineteenth century or the Zen poets of the Tang Dynasty, we must remember that we're talking about *dead* poets. This is not to disparage them. Far from it. As we'll see later in this book, we need those old poets perhaps even more than we realize. But we must understand that they aren't *our* poets.

Our poets breathe the same air we do and wake up to the same headlines on *Huffington Post* and to the same talking heads on *Morning Joe*. Like us, our poets cope with the same realities people have always coped with—the universals of human existence—but they also cope with realities that have never existed before. There *are* new things under the sun: Google, Amazon, ebooks, texting, iPads and iPods, Praline Frappuccinos, GPS, smart phones and smart bombs, designer drugs and designer dogs, reality TV, nuclear terrorism, active-shooter drills, HIV/AIDS, drones, shrinking polar ice caps, ecosystem collapse, vanishing species, corporate oligarchs, Black Lives Matter, and so much more. And our best poets are writing about all of that.[3]

Unless you believe that poets writing now, this year, this moment, are every bit as good as those classic poets of the past—and unless you're reading what our poets write—you will have no idea about how to write poetry. Being a contemporary writer means being a contemporary reader.

At conferences, I sometimes encounter aspiring poets who can't name a single living poet. One young man declared that no good poetry has been written since the time of Wordsworth, though I doubt he'd read any poets since Wordsworth. One woman told me she'd written more than two hundred poems, an astonishing feat, she felt, since she hadn't read any poetry since grade school. She asked, "Should I be *reading* poetry?" I find such people energizing because I'm free to share my favorites, and it excites me to think how much these people have to look forward to. I'm a preacher for poems.

Some readers insist that modern poetry is too hard, which is a sure sign they haven't read much of it. Sure, modern poetry is sometimes hard, but to understand anything, football or accounting, for instance, one must pay careful attention to it, to learn the rules and understand the nuances. Or perhaps *hard* isn't the right word. Poet E. E. Cummings (1894–1962) said, "Poetry is what's *different*."[4] Open a copy of *The New Yorker* or *The Atlantic*, and by and large you'll find the poets published there don't speak "poetry" at all, but plain English in a heart-to-heart, though often a quirky or oblique way—*different*. The trick is to read slowly.

People who insist that poetry is hard should probably not try writing it. Either they have a hard time concentrating, or, more than likely, they are anxious about encountering the disturbing, the embarrassing, the unfamiliar, of sitting and pondering for more time than it takes to read an internet headline. More than sixty years ago, American poet Randall Jarrell (1914–1965) wrote: "The poet lives in a world whose newspapers and magazines and books and motion pictures and radio stations and television stations have destroyed, in a great many people, even the capacity for understanding real poetry, real art of any kind."[5] Imagine what Jarrell would have thought of our digital age.

Reading a poem is risky, even dangerous. It's like striking up a conversation with a stranger, someone who is clearly *not* like you. Who knows what could happen?

The Stranger on the Bus

In fact, I've made this anxiety into a useful exercise.

Try this: find a recent poem by a living poet, one you haven't yet read. Then imagine you are sitting next to a stranger on a cross-town bus, a person who is a little … let's say … odd, perhaps shabbily or eccentrically dressed.

Now, read the poem aloud. Do it slowly and with expression, pretending all the while that it's a monologue delivered to you alone by your seatmate on the bus. Pretend that person is saying, "Hey, you know, here's what I think …" and then read the poem. Try to catch the significance of what this stranger is saying. Your job is to understand the person's background and intuit the reasons that person is reciting this weird monologue to you. The poem might be awkward or aggressive, complex or naïve, penetrating or impenetrable, sweet or sarcastic. If a line doesn't make sense, back up and read it again. Sometimes strangers repeat themselves.

Sometimes a poem is addressed to someone other than the reader, to a spouse or a deceased friend or a parent or God or to everyone or no one in particular, but that makes this bus encounter all the more bizarre. It would be a memorable experience, but if it really happened, you would tell that story for the rest of your life, reconstructing the odd sequence of words that this odd person strung oddly together.

A good poem is like that. You'll think about it later, and perhaps for a long time.

The point is to read, read carefully, and reread, not sentence by sentence or even phrase by phrase, but word by word. How do they go together? What do they say, and what do they hint at? Poetry, as Juan Ramón Jiménez says, is "the almost said,"[6] so you have to look deep. In the words of Palestinian-American poet Naomi Shihab Nye (b. 1952), you need to find the "words under the words."[7]

It's that easy, and it's that hard, but if you're serious about writing poetry, that bus is the only one that will take you there.

Honest Poetry

Some Christians mistakenly think that the current poetry establishment is hostile to religious people, which is, by and large, nonsense. Every journal and book publisher has its own personality and preferences, of course (some want feminist poems, some want rhymed verse, some want gothic howls, and so on), but if they share any intractable prejudice, it's against *bad* poetry.

Hundreds of good living poets who identify as Christian publish in the literary journals; to name just a few (in alphabetical order): Wendell Berry, Scott Cairns, Annie Dillard, Stu Dybek, Louise Erdrich, Dana Gioia, Mark Jarman, Kimberly Johnson, Mary Karr, John Leax, D. S. Martin, Kathleen Norris, Eric Pankey, Brian Phipps, Debra Reinstra, Tania Runyan, Luci Shaw, Kim Stafford, Nancy Willard, Paul Willis, Christian Wiman, Li Young-Lee, Jane Zwart … Most of them write from implicit perspectives of faith. They represent Catholics, Protestants, Orthodox—and the entirely unorthodox.

But of course, listing Christian poets is not the point—it is most particularly *not* the point. A good poem, *any* good poem, whether written by a Christian or not, has the potential of being an "inspired" text, a chapter in "the Third Testament," as Malcolm Muggeridge called it, a vivid reflection of God's creation in written form. The irony is that nonbelieving poets, if they write honestly, can't escape being conduits of God's truth. In the fifth century, Saint Augustine wrote:

> We ought not to give up music because of the superstition of the heathen, if we can derive anything from it that is of use … to lay hold upon spiritual things.… For we ought not to refuse to learn letters because they say that Mercury discovered them; nor because they have dedicated temples to Justice and Virtue, … ought we on that account to forsake justice and virtue. Nay, but let every good and true Christian understand that wherever truth may be found, it belongs to his Master.[8]

While at a Christian writers conference one time, I peppered my talk with quotations from one of my favorite poets without disclosing who it was, quotations that moved and impressed the attendees. At the end, I asked if anyone had guessed who the poet was, and I gave them a hint: though long deceased, he is now the bestselling poet in both the US and Iraq (this was during the second Gulf War). After a number of wrong guesses, I revealed that the poet was Jelaluddin Rumi, the thirteenth-century Sufi Muslim poet, as translated and adapted by American poet Coleman Barks (b. 1937). There was an audible gasp. While there are passages in Rumi's poems I don't understand, what I *do* understand is that Rumi's love for God was so intense, joyful, uninhibited, and original that it makes most Christian poets seem bland by comparison.

The corollary is that dishonest, mawkish, sing-songy poems, especially when written by religious people, no matter how well-meaning, have nothing of interest to say—about anything. God speaks a thousand times more clearly through an honest poem by a pot-smoking agnostic than through a false poem by a Bible-toting humbug.

The Commerce of Poetry

There's a hardcore economic aspect to all this conversation about poetry reading as well. The reason publishers don't publish more poetry (and may not publish *your* poetry in the future) is that it doesn't sell well. Publishers have to make money, and poems are not as much a part of the culture today as they were in the 1960s or the 1860s. But let me share some raw truths:

- If everyone who wrote just *one* poem this year were to buy just *one* book of poetry by a living poet, the publishers would raise a corporate eyebrow.
- If everyone who wrote a poem bought *two* books of poetry, bookstores would have to double their allotted shelf space.
- If everyone who wrote a poem bought just *four* books by living poets this year, *Time* magazine would run a cover story on "The Great Poetry Revival," and even people who don't write poetry would start buying it and reading it.

For far less than the price of a Netflix subscription, we could create a literary revolution. A new book by a living poet costs about as much as two lattes at Starbucks.

And don't scrimp. Don't buy ninety-nine-cent ebooks for your Kindle or view free poetry pages online (though there are lots of good sites that let you do this). That's cheating. It cheapens poetry as a whole. Spend *real* money on *real* print books. If you have one area in life in which to splurge, make it books of poetry. Are they piling up in stacks along your walls? Good. Are you starting to line your shelves two rows deep? It's about time. Read and support living poets (and, when you have money left over, dead poets need your support too). You *have* to do this. It's important.

If you don't know where to start, then here's a reading list. Look online to find who the following award winners are and order books of their poetry (the current winners, as of the publication date of this book, are shown in parentheses):

- The US poet laureate (Tracy K. Smith). Make it a habit buy at least one volume by every new poet laureate.
- The winner of the most recent Pulitzer Prize for poetry (Frank Bidart)
- The winner of the most recent National Book Award for Poetry (also Frank Bidart)
- The recipient of this year's Academy of American Poets Fellowship (Martín Espada)
- The current winner of Bollingen Prize for Poetry (Jean Valentine)
- To discover younger, less established poets, find the most recent author in the Yale Series of Younger Poets (Yanyi)

Or go to a good bookstore and browse. Although the "big-box" bookstores like Barnes & Noble are ubiquitous, new, progressive literary bookshops are popping up all around the country, and most of them have great selections of poetry. Then, buy books by living poets—even if it's just the cover or the title that intrigues you. Buying poetry is essential right now, since many of the larger chain stores are reducing their stock, leaving only Shakespeare's *Sonnets* and Elizabeth Barrett Browning's *Sonnets from the Portuguese*—perennial sellers that nobody reads.

Next, read and subscribe to at least one good literary journal, like *Ploughshares*, *Prairie Schooner*, *The Threepenny Review*, or *The Kenyon Review*. There are scores of them out there. There are even some specifically for Christians: *Image Journal*, *Ruminate*, *Relief*, *Rock and Sling*, *First Things*, *Time of Singing*, *The Windhover*, and many more. And those will become the journals to which you'll start sending your own poetry. Every time you go to the library or to the bookstore, flip to the poems in the latest issue of *The New Yorker*, *The Atlantic*, or *Harper's Magazine*. And be sure to familiarize yourself with *Poetry* magazine from the Poetry Foundation; it is the clearing house for the best poets writing today.

Doing all this will prove to you that the present, not the 1960s—or the 1690s—is the great age of poetry. It always has been and always will be—because it's *now*. As the children outside Saint Augustine's garden chanted, "Take up and read; take up and read."[9]

And do this as a simple exercise: this year, resolve to read *fifty* poems by living poets for every *one* poem you write.

If that seems too burdensome … then your assignment is to read a *hundred*.

Exercises

- Whether you already read contemporary poets or not, go to the bookstore and purchase at least one poetry book by a living poet. It's the "life cycle of poetry." No one will buy your poetry in the future if you aren't buying theirs now.
- Try the stranger-on-the-bus exercise in which you pretend the stranger is reciting a poem to you, as if it were a monologue that catches you by surprise. Read it out loud. Then read it again.

- Most poets don't just write poems, they speak them. Find some of your own old poems and recite them as if you were the stranger on the bus.
- *Poem assignment*: Pick a new poem that you've read recently. Imitate the way that poet writes—the voice, the style, the way the lines are broken. If you don't have an idea for a new poem, then pick a familiar nursery rhyme, and try recasting as that poet would have written it.

Reading

Helpful Resources—Anthologies of Classic and Contemporary Poets

- Two anthologies by former poet laureate Billy Collins (b. 1941), *Poetry, 180: A Turning Back to Poetry* (2003) and *180 More: Extraordinary Poems for Every Day* (2005), contain a mix of classic and recent poets as do the following anthologies.
- The anthology by poet Catherine Bowman (b. 1957), *Word of Mouth: Poems Featured on NPR's* All Things Considered (2003), is a good source of excellent recent poems.
- *Poet's Choice* (2006) by poet Edward Hirsch (b. 1950) takes a variety of themes, provides a couple of poems for each theme, and then analyzes the poems in a clear and engaging way.
- Each volume of the Ten Poems Series by Roger Housden (b. 1945) offers insightful essays about ten different poems; they are basically a primer on how to read poetry. Try *Ten Poems to Change Your Life* (2001),

Ten Poems to Set You Free (2003). Also recommended is his anthology *For Lovers of God Everywhere: Poems of the Christian Mystics* (2009).

The poet doesn't invent. He listens.
—Jean Cocteau
(1889–1963)[1]

3
Silence: The Infinite Longing

Words fail us.

We are left with silence.

On September 11, 2001, and in the days that followed, many of us spoke words like *tragedy*, *cataclysm*, *disaster*, and *catastrophe* to express our shock, vulnerability, and outrage. Eventually, those words seemed to dissipate, even as we knew the smoke from those fallen towers, sooner or later, would vanish. It is not because our feelings grew any less intense that those words grew less common; rather, I suspect we acknowledged, if unconsciously, the utter inadequacy of words to capture our feelings and the feelings of an entire nation.

Now, nearly two decades later, there is no greater evidence to both the power and the insufficiency of words than the fact that we refer to that time as the *events* of 9/11. It's a cagey, neutral little word that gathers within its small, impotent soul not just the incidents of that day but all the memories of those inexpressible feelings as well. It's a safe word, one that promises not to reopen wounds but also never to let us forget.

What We Turn To

Two weeks after those "events," Terri Gross interviewed then–US poet laureate Billy Collins (b. 1941) on her *Fresh Air* radio program on NPR. Collins was then, and continues to be, one of the most widely read contemporary American poets. Other than the tragedy itself, this interview is what most stands out in my memory of that grim September. Amid the almost desperate media chatter and constant electronic rehashing, nothing, in my opinion, even remotely compared in elegance, simplicity, and wisdom to that single twenty-minute conversation.

While admitting that no words were adequate, Collins observed that during those bleak, grieving days, the nation was experiencing a sudden outpouring of poetry. People who had seldom written a line were now writing poems to cope with their grief. These were read at memorial services, on television, and in churches; they were shared at work, stuffed into chain-link fences, and published in local newspapers. Several 9/11 poetry anthologies were published. Collins said that in his capacity as poet laureate he even experienced a sharp uptick in the number of invitations he received to speak.

To him, this interest in poetry seemed significant. As he told Terry Gross, "In a time of national crisis, we don't turn to the novel. We don't say we should all go out and see a movie.... We turn to poetry."[2]

When Terri Gross asked him to suggest specific poems that might be of comfort, he said, "Any poem," because true poetry provides a way for us to "ritualize our grief." When she pressed him again, he said, "The Psalms." It was a profound declaration.

Prayer

I think that interview was the moment I first realized that poem-making is a form of prayer, that writing poetry, and speaking it interiorly or aloud, is a way of praying. When words fail us, paradoxically, we turn to poetry with the same inner gesture we use for prayer. Although we often don't feel poetic when we pray, especially in times of crisis, we still practice a kind of prayerfulness as we write.

The conventional way is to write poems that are themselves prayers. As a genre, the prayer poem not only has a long history but is familiar to the adherents of most religions. King David of Israel made no distinction between his prayers and his poems—particularly amid his tumultuous times. His name appears as the author of almost half of the Psalms, which are, after all, poems sung as prayers, complete with their own complex prosody. Although many scholars dispute their authorship, most of us have a hard time imagining anyone other than the biblical David intoning lines like, "Create in me a clean heart, O God" or "I will take refuge in the shadow of your wings."[3] As Billy Collins suggested, they are unsurpassed as poems and as prayers, and for millennia, Jews and Christians have prayed them as their own. Even Jesus prayed them as his own. Monk and poet Thomas Merton (1915–1968) once wrote, "This is the secret of the Psalms. Our identity is hidden in them. In them we find ourselves and God."[4]

Some of the earliest known poems in English were prayers. "Caedmon's Hymn," which dates from the late seventh century, addresses God in such rough-hewn terms as "Gloryfather," "Holy Shaper," and "Middle Earth mankind's Warden."[5]

In the seventeenth century, Anglican priest and poet John Donne (1572–1631) wrote many of his "divine" poems in the form of prayers, as did George Herbert (1593–1663), Henry Vaughan (1621–1695), Thomas Traherne (1636–1674), and John Milton (1608–1674). Poet-priest Robert Herrick (1591–1674) even wrote a poem asking God to forgive him for all the poems he had written that were less than "divine." Later there was William Cowper (1731–1800), Gerard Manley Hopkins (1844–1889), James Weldon Johnson (1871–1938), David Jones (1898–1974), and many others.

Silence

Still, for all that, the prayer poem is a tricky genre. A poem that addresses "God" or "Savior" or "Creator" in the second person can come off sounding sanctimonious and as cloying as a love poem addressed to "my dear." Prayer poems can feel fake—talking to God when you're really talking to the reader—a sort of spiritual ventriloquism. And prayer poems sometimes lean on outworn jargon, pulpit language, King James English. Stale clichés make for stale writing, and stale prayer poems make Caedmon's ancient "Gloryfather" and "Holy Shaper" seem fresh by comparison.

What I suggest, for a short time at least, is that we give up the idea of having to say anything at all, of having to talk our way into a poem. Just stop. Be silent. There is a kind of prayer called "contemplative prayer," which differs from the "petitionary" kind in that it has no agenda, no list of demands, no rote phrases. It seeks communion with God through silence, through waiting.

When we read classic poetry, we are often impressed by the big voices, self-expression writ large. Much good writing is of the confident, booming, prophetic kind, proclamations that echo in the rafters—like kettle drums in the Taj Mahal. We hear such epic voices in Homer and Sophocles, Dante and Donne, Milton and Pope, Allen Ginsberg and Derek Walcott. It's most of the Romantic poets rolled into one. It's Walt Whitman (1819–1892)—especially Whitman—whom G. K. Chesterton satirized with the line "I myself am a complete orchestra."[6]

But even those poets couldn't have written if they hadn't first dropped a bucket into some inner well of quiet. One important thing that poetry and prayer have in common is that they are not so much forms of expression as forms of expectation, of waiting to see what God, who fills the silence, will do next. They are ways of listening.

If you're like me, you're wary of well-meaning people who advise you to "listen to God"—because I'm never sure what that means. I've known people who claim to hear God as an actual spoken voice. Some say that God speaks to them by calling their attention to timely, needful Bible verses. I even knew a man who claimed that he could read God's words like ticker-tape across the insides of his eyelids.

I've never experienced God in those ways.

So what kind of listening am I talking about?

The honest answer is, I don't know. Listening is different for every person, so only you can discover what that means for yourself. But I do know there's something truthful and profound in saying that the silence is nothing more nor less than itself, that it's there, that it's something so vast that we are hardly aware of it, let alone able to comprehend it. It's like the empty space between here and the farthest star. As St. John of the Cross once wrote, "To know with certainty the path you are on, you must close your eyes and walk in darkness."[7]

The silence is not about us, and it is not even about poems. It is, for the spiritual person, about being present. Present with God, who fills that silence and *is* that silence. In whatever way we find ourselves in God's presence, it is important to be there, alone, without theories, without words or agendas, dogmas or doctrines, realizing that we are never beyond that presence even in all the other busy and distracted moments of our lives. Whether we realize it or not, we are, as an anonymous Franciscan once said, "naked before God, alone with the Alone."[8]

What I'm suggesting is that we take advantage of the fact that words *do* fail us. We feel this urge to praise God, to talk with, and sometimes *at*, God. But how effective is all that talking really? How do we feel when someone flatters us all the time, praises us, then makes demands of us, when they talk and talk and never shut up? Most of us, I think, would rather sit silently with a friend than to hear fulsome, insincere praise.

Even in that famous verse from Psalm 46, which begins, "God is our refuge and strength, a very present help in trouble," after the psalmist has rattled on for nine verses in his praise for the Divine, God finally breaks in. God stops the chatter by saying, "Be still …"[9] It reminds me of the wild things in Maurice Sendak's *Where the Wild Things Are*, whom Max tames by saying those same words—"Be still"—and then by "staring into all their yellow eyes without blinking once."[10] God, instead of staring into our yellow eyes, finishes the sentence: "And know that I am God."

It requires a great deal of humility and the ability to put ourselves—as well as our favorite religious notions—aside in order to be still. Those who find this untalkative fellowship with God to be the most meaningful experience in life—and Christians are called to that throughout the Bible—to dwell in that presence. They are called mystics. As writers and poets, we're part of their clan.

But we are also called—like international journalists—to return from that foreign place of silence, bringing back news bulletins in the form of poems. How those bulletins get written is the subject of the next chapter on "Process."

The Discipline of Noticing

Whatever silence, listening, or contemplative prayer mean to you, they are best practiced every day. Writing poetry also works best when it's a habit. Many poets, from the ancient Roman Catullus (c. 84–54 BCE) to the modern American Robert Bly (b. 1926), disciplined themselves to write a poem every day. Emily Dickinson (1830–1886) and Robert Browning (1812–1889) made similar resolutions. William Stafford (1914–1993) would rise every morning, hours before the rest of his family, not for devotions but for the purpose of writing a poem. One each day. Stafford, an American Quaker, wrote poems that exude the early morning quietude of prayer. In him I sense that prayer time and poetry time were one, especially when I read such lines as this from his poem "The Center," "Whenever you breathe God comes in."[11]

Of course, daily discipline can often feel like just going through the motions. It doesn't always feel productive. Stafford, I think, put his finger on the reason when he was asked in an interview how it was possible to write a poem every day. He responded, half-jokingly, "My standards are low."[12]

Many of us don't like to pray because our expectations are impossibly high. We start by thinking we should pray at least an hour every day or that the results should be dramatic and immediate. In the same way, we often have overblown expectations of what our daily writing time should be like. We expect breakthroughs and brilliance. But like Stafford, whether we pray or write, we need to lower our expectations and just be there with God and with the writing. Ninety percent of the work is just showing up.

In such matters, I take a cue from American farmer, activist, and poet Wendell Berry (b. 1934). For three and a half decades he has made it his practice to take a walk every Sunday for the purpose of writing a poem. Few writers have written as much on the subject of work as Berry, so it seems appropriate that he should spend each Sabbath—his day of rest—writing a poem. The best of these are collected in his book *This Day: New and Collected Sabbath Poems* (2013).

I can think of no better characterization of both poetry and prayer than the following lines from one of Berry's Sabbath poems. Though addressed to his wife, the sentiment is as true of our relationship to God:

> Loving you has taught me the infinite
> longing of the self to be given away.[13]

In both prayer and poetry we express the same urge to relinquish, to give ourselves away. Writing a poem is a gift to the reader; it is an act of open-handedness, of generosity. Such writing has nothing to do with preaching or asserting ourselves. It's not witnessing or "sharing the gospel." It's noticing what we notice, perceiving life in the most honest way possible, and, above all, paying attention to the minutiae, the modest unnoticeables. Then we share our noticing with others.

Poetry and prayer overlap. They begin and end in silence, and in between, they share a common language, not of words but of perception, emotion, and mindfulness. They are conversations with someone who is present but unseen—whether God or the imagined reader. And they are solitary practices in which, at their best, we give ourselves to another, which is what Jesus instructed his followers to do in the first place.

Gratitude

Finally, poetry and prayer have one more thing in common, something that Billy Collins mentioned in his interview with Terry Gross. He explained that one of the reasons he loves haiku is because they are miniature expressions of joy, ways of celebrating small, single moments of time. All poetry, he said, is like that, creating "a chapel for the importance of everyday experience." And we desperately need the thing that is contained at the heart of every good poem, which is, in Collins's words, "a prayer of gratitude."

Exercises

- Think about how you pray. Do you pray aloud? Do you verbalize words in your head when you pray silently? Are you comfortable being silent, imagining yourself in God's presence without words at all? If not, try to cultivate silence as a way to clear the mind and open yourself to God's spirit.
- What is your favorite psalm? Try reading it aloud as if it were poetry. What do experience in doing that?
- Set a time limit, perhaps two weeks, and discipline yourself to write something every day. Keep your expectations modest. At the end of two weeks, see what

rises to the top; pick out the best lines and phrases and see what you can make of them. Find dissimilar ideas and find ways to tie them together.

- *Poem assignments*: Try writing your own psalm in the style of whatever Bible version you use. Or try "translating," or paraphrasing, one of the Bible psalms into contemporary language, replacing any antiquated imagery with modern equivalents. Make it so modern that the psalm would be almost unrecognizable to most readers.

Reading

Helpful Resources

- Poet and activist Robert McDowell's *Poetry as a Spiritual Practice: Reading, Writing, and Using Poetry in Your Daily Rituals, Aspirations, and Intentions* (2008) explores the connection between writing and spirituality.
- *Contemplative Prayer* (1969) by monk and poet Thomas Merton (1915–1968), although not about writing, is as profound an introduction to silence and prayer as you will find.
- You can find some beautiful, magnificent prayers, some in poetic form, in Anglican bishop George Appleton's anthology *The Oxford Book of Prayer* (Oxford Univ. Press, 1985).
- *Poem assignment:* Read at least half a dozen psalms; then write your own.

Classic Poets

- Two poets who seemed to be able to make every poem into a prayer are seventeenth-century poet-divines George Herbert (1593–1633) and Thomas Traherne

(c. 1638–1674). Many editions of their poetry are available.

- For a different approach to prayer poems, be sure to find the whimsical but profound *Prayers from the Ark* and *The Creatures' Choir* by French poet Carmen de Bernos de Gasztold (1919–1995), which were translated into English by novelist Rumer Godden.

Contemporary Poets

- *This Day: New and Collected Sabbath Poems: 1979–2012* (2013) by Wendell Berry (b. 1934) is a good introduction to his poetry.
- Writer and former radio host Garrison Keillor (b. 1942) compiled an excellent anthology of poems written in response to crises, personal and national, by both classic and contemporary poets: *Good Poems for Hard Times* (Penguin, 2005).

I have to write what's difficult,
otherwise it is difficult to write.
—Mirza Ghalib
(1797–1869)[1]

4

Process: The Empty Page

At a certain point, silence manifests itself in a physical form—the blank page. It is now no longer just silence; it's sitting on our desk or on our screen, waiting for something to happen. The time for listening is over. It's time to feel our way forward, like searching for the light switch in a dark room, to illuminate what's going on inside us. Things take shape in that void: unexpected ideas, curious connections, silly notions, and emotional burdens, often unexpressed, unheeded, and unnoticed until now. Something inside us is burning to get out, and we need to pay attention to it. As Scottish poet George Mackay Brown (1921–1996) wrote, the poet's task is the "interrogation of silence."[2]

Our job now becomes a Promethean one—to steal fire from that other world and to bring it back, in the shape of words, to our own.

Seeking the Poem

Each time I visit our local natural-history museum, I'm drawn to one particular diorama. Like a toddler with an iPad, I'm mesmerized. Even though I've seen it a dozen times, it never fails to startle.

In the life-size scene, three wolves are tracking through the knee-deep snow of a high ridge. The night is vast and blue-black and speckled with stars, which makes it seem as if the air itself would shatter if so much as a twig snapped. The wolves crouch low. They've spotted something, and the scene catches them at a moment of veering aside, their lips curling in hunger. Down the ridge, across a wide mist-covered valley, and just perceptible on the far slope, a herd of whitetail deer lurk at the edge of the snow-dusted pines. Some of the deer have picked up the wolf-scent, and a few are beginning to run. The azure coldness of the scene catches my breath, and the harshness of that hunger seems so bitter. It is a gripping image of desire—that numbing, barren landscape between predator and prey.

The scene approximates the feeling I get when I face a blank sheet of paper or an empty computer screen (I write in both formats)—the snow-white page, the trackless expanse of possibility. If you write, you know that feeling.

Some poets tell me they never lack for subjects. Just be ready, they say, and the ideas will come. Their brains are always teeming. They're lucky. My mind too teems with ideas, but once I have eliminated the trite, the sentimental, the clichéd, the obvious, and the melodramatic, I feel like those wolves on that ridge—aching and empty.

In one of his *Essais*, Montaigne (1533–1592), the sixteenth-century French writer, tells the story of a friend who claimed to have so many original thoughts bubbling up in his brain that he couldn't write fast enough to get them down on paper. So the great essayist, who had once devised his own form of shorthand, suggested that his friend dictate to him so that he might record every brilliant idea. So it was agreed. Montaigne readied his quills and paper, and looked up expectantly. His friend went blank. He couldn't think of a single thing.

The story is a portrait of myself every time I open my notebook to start a new poem, pen poised above the page—

except I'm both the amused Montaigne and the fatuous friend rolled into one.

For me, the hardest work is not the writing itself but overcoming something akin to agoraphobia, the fear of open spaces—all that vast anticipation, where the first step is unmarked. It is as though God allows us a minuscule glimpse into what "in the beginning" must have felt like—to face creatively something that is "without form, and void" and where darkness is "upon the face of the deep."

The Already Written

A few Christmases ago, I spent an evening with a professional violinist—a talented woman, whose late father was a friend of mine and a fine poet. She agreed to confer a blessing on my own scratchy fiddle by playing the opening of Bach's Partita No. 3. It sounded like heaven. "How do you do that?" I asked her. "How do you just pick up a violin and do that?"

She said, "I know I can do it when I can play the whole thing in my mind." She can visualize it, finger for finger, note for note.

I said, "I wish I could do that with poems, but writing a poem feels like learning the violin from scratch every time."

"But I'm playing someone else's music," she said. "I don't have to write it."

And that gave me an inkling of an idea. What if I don't need to create the poem from scratch? What if my job is, like a violinist's, to be the one who expresses something that is already there? If we take for granted the idea that God knows everything that will happen in the future, that he's omniscient and prescient, then all my poems and your poems are, in a sense, already written. Our job, like the violinist's, is just to "play" them.

Having been raised a sometime Methodist, I tend not to lean on concepts of predestination, but in this case, I suppose I'm sort of a limited predestinarian. What if I were to assume that the music of the poem is already humming somewhere, waiting to play itself through me? It's a spiritual act, an act of trust, a method of getting myself out of the way so that something true and inevitable can happen. Michelangelo wrote somewhere that every block of stone already has a statue hiding inside it. The sculptor's job is to dig it out.

Process

The wolves on the ridge don't create their prey. The deer are already there. So how do we cross that space between the dreamed-of and the done? We already have the idea or the emotional pressure, but how do we discover the poem that is waiting to be written?

The answer is *process*. Everyone has a process, even if that process is just to sit down and start writing. Just do it, as the ads say. The wolves just start running. It's what they do.

But for some people, that's not so easy; they need a nudge to commit to that first word, that first line, a kernel of an idea for the poem. The nudge may be different for everyone, and it may even be different from poem to poem, but it's helpful to know which nudges work best for you.

Poet Richard Hugo (1923–1982) called his process "the triggering town." He would imagine himself walking into an unfamiliar town, somewhere in the rural northwest, perhaps at night. In his mind, he paced along the empty streets and sidewalks, catching glimpses of people in their houses where the windows shimmered with blue light. And he thought about what he would observe. What would he think and feel? Who were these strangers and what were their stories? And the poem started from there, from that simple thought experiment.

Your goal is to find your own triggering town.

Here are just a few approaches to process that many poets I know have tried and found useful:

- *Use Prompts*: You can find any number of books that give you suggestions for writing poems, offering simple ideas like "Describe the way your hand works" or "Write about one of your earliest memories." Before you write, think about how that particular prompt arouses something inside you. What associations does it have for you? (See "Readings" at the end of this chapter for some books of prompts.)

- *Journal*: Your own life experiences are the best prompts of all. Keep a journal as a way to remind yourself that even the smallest events in your life are often full of drama and interest. The goal of a journal is to make your life into the best "prompt book" imaginable.
- *Practice Ekphrasis*: Visit a museum or study a book of art, and contemplate a painting. Write about what you perceive. That process is called *ekphrasis*. Sometimes by focusing on something outside yourself, you discover what's inside. Evoke in words the feeling the landscape painter was trying to convey, or imagine who the person in the portrait really is. Go beyond the scene itself to envision the context, the setting, what happened before and after. Fill in the gaps. Try doing this with music, sculpture, film, and photographs. Recollect scenes from your past and visualize them as if they were works of art or short films. And write about them.
- *Be a Magpie*: Collect words and short phrases from your reading and shuffle them around enough to make them your own. *The Wasteland* by T. S. Eliot (1888–1965) is full of such borrowings. As he once wrote in his book *The Sacred Wood*:

> Immature poets imitate; mature poets steal; bad poets deface what they take, and good poets make it into something better, or at least something different. The good poet welds his theft into a whole of feeling which is unique, utterly different from that from which it was

> torn; the bad poet throws it into something which has no cohesion. A good poet will usually borrow from authors remote in time, or alien in language, or diverse in interest.[3]

Note that this idea is *not* an invitation to plagiarize. It is, rather, a way of allowing other sources to prime the pump of your creativity.

- *Overhear*: Tune in to the bits of conversation all around you—in the grocery line, at the PTA, in a restaurant, in the cubicle at work. I once overheard a man in a café telling his friend about seeing what he believed to be an angel. He said the glowing apparition stood at the foot of his bed and shifted side to side "like a statue on wheels." The scene was so irresistible that I later made it into a poem. Just yesterday, my six-year-old neighbor girl said, "Spring is a thrill sport. You never know what's going to happen next." There's a poem there.
- *Free Associate*: Writing several stream-of-consciousness pages. Let one word suggest the next without overthinking anything—whatever odd words and combinations come to mind—until something glows. Rescue the most intriguing lines and thoughts from the resulting word-heap, and construct a poem around them. The hope is that the randomness will suggest ideas and juxtapositions that you wouldn't have thought of otherwise. I have been amazed to find, at times, that whole poems rise from those embers—and often they are the poems that express my strongest, deepest emotions. Here's the middle section of a poem I wrote about dying, all of which came spontaneously:

> The pilgrim merges with the way,
> loses himself in leaves and moss,

counts instances of time
on the points of frost and dies.

His final ecstasy is this:
one dark tree falling slowly

through the arms of others.[4]

The transition from the pilgrim to the frost to the dark tree was unthought-out, free-associative, but I liked the way it flowed. And I still have no idea what it means to count "instances of time / on the points of frost," but I love the oblique evocativeness of the image.

- *Speak in Tongues*: No, not glossolalia, but try writing in the voice of someone other than yourself. Practice empathy. Settle on some person, either real or imaginary, and get inside their head and see the world from their peep-hole on the universe. Then start talking. It's a good way to get outside yourself and, in an odd way, to find out more about yourself. Mimic the many voices inside you and all around you.
- *Get Moving*: Rather than walking through an imaginary triggering town like Richard Hugo's, take an actual walk. Many writers find that thoughts flow more easily once they get moving. Some writers even compose aloud as they walk. The Japanese have an art form, called *haibun*, which is the writing of a haiku journal as you walk or travel. I have written any number of poems while walking around the track at the YMCA.

Process is a way to begin chipping the sculpture out of the stone. Once you've identified a piece of poem, just a corner, the odds of digging out the rest vastly improve. After it has taken the hint of a shape in the mind, the poem tends to flow, if not easily, then at least organically. You've started running after the deer. With patience, you will not return empty-handed from that foray into silence. You will learn to move out of the way and let the poem work itself out. Like the violinist, you learn to visualize your piece from beginning to end so that, with practice, you can pick up the pen and write. Listen to where the poem wants to go.

If you're an ever-flowing fountain of poems, then count yourself lucky. It's a gift, so cherish it. But if you're like most, poems come slowly. They are work and involve waiting. So learn to relish the hunger. Stare out over that valley and experience that distance and that hunger honestly. But also trust that you will not starve this time, just as you didn't starve last time. Even if you don't succeed, another poem will be there eventually.

But if you don't make that dash, again and again, you will most assuredly starve.

Exercises

- Have you thought about your process? What has helped you write poems in the past? Choose one of the processes from the list above and experiment with it for a week. If it doesn't work, then try another one for a week. Persist.
- *Poem assignment.* Try constructing a poem from the ground up, with no plan to begin with. Do this: Think of a word. Just one. A common word. Nothing exotic. Hold the word in your mind, then write it down. Then wait for a phrase to suggest itself around that word. A short phrase, no more than that. If it makes no sense, consider it a gift. You do not need to make sense at this point. If it makes no sense but is beautiful, then

you have been given a wonderful gift indeed. Build that phrase into a short sentence, and again, don't bother making a lot of sense. Write a second sentence. Let it grow from the first. Or not. They can simply be together and resonate. Did I already say, "Feel *no* obligation to make sense"? At some point, you might continue the writing by interpreting what you've written as if you were someone interpreting "tongues," as Paul speaks of in Corinthians 12:10.

Reading

Helpful Resources

- One of the best books about coping with the empty page—about starting a new work of art of any kind—is psychotherapist and creativity-coach Eric Maisel's *Fearless Creating: A Step-by-Step Guide to Starting and Completing Your Work of Art* (1995). The exercises in Maisel's book are particularly helpful in finding your process.
- I found Julia Cameron's practical and popular "life workbooks" *The Artist's Way: A Spiritual Path to Higher Creativity* (twenty-fifth anniversary edition 2016) and *A Vein of Gold: A Journey to Your Creative Heart* (1997) to be helpful.
- Check out Richard Hugo's helpful essays in his book *Triggering Town* (2010).
- An excellent book of prompts: *Writing Without the Muse: Sixty Beginning Exercises for the Creative Writer* (1999) by American poet Beth Baruch Joselow (b. 1948). One of the most fun books of prompts is *The Pocket Muse: Ideas and Inspirations for Writing* (2001) by fiction writer Monica Wood.

- General inspiration: Susan Shaughnessy's *Walking on Alligators: A Book of Meditations for Writers* (1993) and Bonni Goldberg's *Room to Write: Daily Invitations to a Writer's Life* (1996)

Classic Poets

- Writing ekphrastic poetry is a popular technique. One of my favorites is William Carlos Williams's *Pictures from Brueghel and Other Poems* (1962).
- As a supplement to Richard Hugo's *Triggering Town*, treat yourself to reading some of his poetry: *Selected Poems* (Norton, 1979). Notice how his "triggering town" concept might have inspired him in some of his poems.

Contemporary Poets

- Twenty-one of Lawrence Ferlinghetti's poems about paintings have been collected, along with color reproductions of many of the paintings, in the volume *When I Look at Pictures* (Peregrine Smith Books, 1990). As a painter himself, Ferlinghetti's approach is unusually intriguing.
- Poet Marilyn Chandler McEntyre (b. 1949) has written three elegant four-color books inspired by paintings: *In Quiet Light: Poems on Vermeer's Women* (Eerdmans, 2000) and *Drawn to the Light: Poems on Rembrandt's Religious Paintings* (Eerdmans, 2003); and *The Color of Light: Poems on Van Gogh's Late Paintings* (Eerdmans, 2007).
- I also recommend Walter Wangerin Jr.'s *The Absolute, Relatively Inaccessible* (Cascade, 2017), which contains many ekphrastic poems.

Standing midway between the heavens
and the earth,
the poet sees the glistening mysteries.
—Lu Chi[1]

5

Creativity: From the Big Bang to the Big Kahuna

The year was 1977. NASA launched two probes into space with the intention of having them soar past Jupiter and the outer planets, snapping photos as they went—not unlike tourists on a double-decker bus rumbling past Westminster Abbey. But unlike those tourists, the two Voyager spacecraft held one-way tickets only, for their path led straight out of the solar system and into deep space.

Twenty years later, by the late 1990s, the spacecraft had zipped past Pluto's orbit at the speed of 38,000 miles per hour, and even now, the probes continue to send signals back to earth, enabling scientists to monitor the point at which the sun's magnetic field stops and the "interstellar wind" begins. I have no idea what "interstellar wind" is, but it is nothing short of imagination candy. The two spacecraft are the farthest human-made objects from earth, and scientists are confident that they will still be zooming along well after our own sun turns into a red giant and burns up the earth, as it's forecast to do some five billion years from now.

Cosmic Talking Tube

Most people remember the Voyager project for another reason. Aboard each of those spacecraft, scientists placed golden twelve-inch records, complete with pictographic instructions on how they should be played should they ever be discovered by some hyper-intelligent extraterrestrial beings. Those discs piqued the imaginations of millions around the world, for they contained sound recordings representative of Planet Earth; included were such aural artifacts as whale song, ocean surf, bird calls, and animal growls. The recordings offer samples of music from around the world, including Bach, Javanese gamelan, gospel/bluesman Blind Willie Johnson, and 1950s rocker Chuck Berry, as well as spoken samples of fifty-five languages—all of it, in part, the brainchild of popular astronomer Carl Sagan. (You may remember the old *Saturday Night Live* skit in which NASA scientists receive the first signals back from an alien civilization. When they decipher the message, it reads: "Send more Chuck Berry.")

Of course, the whole concept was quixotic at best. Who knows if anyone is "out there," but assuming they are, the distances involved are staggering. Traveling, as it is, at a rate of more than 300 million miles a year, Voyager 2 (which has now taken the lead) won't even approach our nearest celestial neighbor for another 40,000 years. That's 12 trillion miles away.

To get a picture of how large a trillion is, consider this: a watch that ticks every second will tick a *million* times in eleven-and-a-half days. It will take that same watch thirty-two years to tick a *billion* times. How long will it take for that watch to tick a *trillion* times? 32,000 years. And it would take 380,000 years to tick 12 trillion times.

As I thought about Voyager recently, I wondered what poetry samples among the fifty-five languages were included on those golden discs. The answer startled me. None. No poetry. Just nature sounds, spoken greetings, and music. Forget Chuck Berry, I thought, send Wendell!

It seemed odd. I had long assumed that maybe Shakespeare was on the disc—or a bit of Homer or Dante or Cervantes at the very least. But I was wrong. I was reminded of those "talking tubes" on the playground; a sort of tall tubular funnel sticks out of the ground on one end of the play area and another at the other end, and through the underground tube that connects them, you can talk in a clear whisper to someone sixty feet away. Of course, after you say, "Hellooo, how are youuu?" and the other person says, "Okaaay, how are youuu?" you run out of words to say.

Without poetry, it seems to me, Voyager is nothing more than an expensive way of saying, "Hellooo, how are youuu?" into the tube of the cosmos, which, while still a noble endeavor, makes one feel sort of lonely, especially when we're not even sure anyone else is on the playground.

The Library of Post-Nuclear-Holocaust Studies

A few years ago, before pondering Voyager, I had a dream that filled me with that same hollow feeling. In it, I visited an unusual library called "the Library of Post-Nuclear-Holocaust Studies." Having been raised during the Cold War, I still have those nightmares.

Now, unlike Voyager, this library was not a repository of the best of human culture. Rather, it shelved only those books that would be useful to humans in rebuilding the world from scratch—after humans had destroyed it. The librarian bragged that the building housed "the world's largest collection of self-help books." It also contained books about architecture and agronomy, mechanics, animal husbandry, medicine, and so on. The structure itself was bomb- and radiation-proof, guaranteed to be the only thing left standing when the Doomsday Clock read five seconds after midnight.

In the dream, I thought, *So, what about poetry? Surely, they must have poetry in the collection.* So, true child of the pre-computer era that I am, I thumbed through the card catalog. Remember three-by-five cards? I couldn't even find the Ps for Poetry. So I checked the microfiche files, only to find them indecipherable. A single computer sat on a desk against the wall, but someone was using it. In the dream I even thought, "Now I wish I'd memorized the Library of Congress classification numbers!" (I've since checked—American poetry is PS3600.)

I was stymied. Is it possible that there will be no poetry to read if anyone happens to survive the nuclear holocaust? How can we rebuild civilization without Shakespeare and Homer and Dante—or Lao Tzu or Rumi or Basho or Blake or Han Shan or Yeats and so many more? Who would even *want* to survive?

But just before waking, a thought occurred—a blessed, joyful, powerful, happy thought—and this is the point: The poetry for rebuilding civilization is not found on any shelf in the world. It's found inside you and inside me and inside everyone who writes poetry. Right now. Waiting to be written. As William Butler Yeats (1865–1939) wrote in his poem "Lapis Lazuli," "All things fall and are built again / And those that build them again are gay."[2] You and I are the rebuilders, not Shakespeare or Dante. The poetry of the past doesn't build the world of the future. The poetry being written right now does.

And with that thought, I woke up.

You Are the Miracle

The Voyager spacecraft and the Library of Post-Nuclear-Holocaust Studies are distant echoes of all those strange old myths in which human culture is funneled through a tiny threadlike passage from an old world to a new one. They are variants of the Noah's Ark story—and its Babylonian cousin (which could be called Utnapishtim's Ark) and the Greek version (Deucalion's Ark). A human remnant passes from the tired old wicked world to establish a revitalized new one—bearing with them the raw essentials for starting fresh. Dozens of science-fiction movies and novels take that theme for their premise—the seeding of a new civilization.

Ultimately, as world-famous psychiatrist and writer Carl Jung once pointed out, these stories are so deeply ingrained in our psyches because they are archetypal births. Like Noah and Utnapishtim and Deucalion, each of us survives a risky journey from our mother's wombs, through an amniotic sea, only to discover a new world upon birth. And we carry just the essentials with us—which is not much more than our singular genetic code.

Remember my watch that takes 380,000 years to tick 12 trillion times? Well, if my math is correct, you are just one of 80 trillion possible egg-sperm combinations your parents could have conceived. So, imagine a big roulette wheel with 80 trillion numbers on it! Just by being born, by being here, you won the largest jackpot in the history of the universe.

Or look at it this way: on that eternally ticking watch, 80 trillion seconds ago was around the year 2.5 million BCE, not long after the earliest hominids were thought to have begun toddling upright around Africa. Now, pinpoint a single second somewhere along that vast timeline and ask someone to guess which second you're thinking of. Those are the odds that you would be you. But here you are. You are a miracle in the flesh. And you brought with you your particular genes that somehow or other have predisposed you to write poems. And those divinely given genes have predisposed you that way for a reason. You want to write poems because you were meant to write poems.

Rebuilding the World

It's a miracle that we are even here. But, if we are aboard that ark of time, what world is it that we've been called upon to rebuild?

The fact is that all of us living now, whether we write poetry or not, have lost the entire world to an ongoing cataclysmic flood—that is, the flood of complacency, of neglect, and of taking the miracle of life for granted, of letting our perceptions, and those of everyone else in the world, calcify and die. Old values and old meanings are lost daily. We look around and the world no longer shimmers with God's light in our eyes, and it no longer vibrates with the singing of the celestial spheres in our ears, because we—all of us—have grown too accustomed to the light and too deaf to that heavenly song. We humans, as a species, lose our world every day to the nuclear winter of inattention, distraction, and preoccupation by forgetting the simple but awe-inspiring thisness of being alive, of being here.

Our first job as a poet is to wake up. Our second job is to wake up those around us.

There's a solid rationale for poetry not being on Voyager. Because in the absence of humans, poetry makes no sense. It doesn't need to be in the Library of Post-Nuclear-Holocaust Studies. Nor does it need to be aboard the ark. Because you and I are aboard the ark right now, and we are called upon to be the re-creators of a world that has become so common, so overfamiliar, that most people even fail to notice it anymore. In his "Defence of Poetry," Romantic poet Percy Bysshe Shelley (1792–1822) wrote that poetry "creates anew the universe, after it has been annihilated in our minds by the recurrence of impressions blunted by reiteration."[3]

When you think about it, "creating anew the universe" is what the great poetic movements of the past have done. Whether the ancient oral and epic traditions; the Japanese haikuists (the Danrin movement) and the English Metaphysical poets of the seventeenth century; the European Romantics and the French Symbolists and the Transcendentalists of the nineteenth; the Irish Renaissance, the Modernists, the Harlem Renaissance, the Beats, and the Confessionalists of the twentieth; and so many more—all of them endeavored to restore the universe after the old truths had been destroyed and old meanings had been drowned. The job of the poet is to rescue the sadly discarded world. "People do not invent," wrote Yeats, "they remember."[4]

To respond to this calling, we need to read the great poets and thinkers and philosophers and saints of the past. Just as Dante read the Greek and Roman classics; just as Shakespeare read Plutarch and Holinshed, and Keats read the Greek myths; just as Tennyson read the Arthurian legends, Yeats read Irish folklore, and T. S. Eliot read Dante and the French Symbolists, we need to read the classic literature of the past. We can't even begin to know the world that *is* until we know the world that *was*.

Riding the Wave

While we are building that outer world of culture and tradition and ancient truth with our poetry, we are building an inner world as well.

According to those who are supposed to know, the universe is expanding rapidly, and in my opinion, our own creativity is a tiny part of that expanding universe. We, these generations upon generations of improbable human beings, devising new and improbable poems and rebuilding the worlds that others have forgotten, are riding the crest of the great creative wave that began with the Big Bang. We're surfing on the edge of the unknown, hot-dogging on the wild surf of eternity. The universe isn't just expanding "out there." It's expanding everywhere, especially here, inside each of us, among us, in the human love that motivates us to share ideas, express emotions, and generate new connections. We are creating an inner world that has never existed before and that we are meant to share with others.

The things you notice that the rest of us take for granted, the stories that are swirling within you, the emotions that have built up inside, the ideas that occur to you, the experiences you have had—all these are the tools you will use to "create anew the universe." Every experience you have is part of that ever-enlarging creation of the universe, and your most interesting experiences will be the seeds of your poems. In that way, you become a continuer, a micro-sustainer of that initial, huge act of Creation. Your own imagination pushes the outer boundary of the universe out just a little farther with each poem.

As fast as Voyager is traveling, it will never catch up to the new poems that will be written this year and every year for the next five billion years, because those poems, those creative moments, are already out there—and in here—on the farthermost edge of the Big Bang, bringing the new into existence.

Although I love the Genesis version of the story of Noah and the Great Flood above all, I have to concede that the Greek version makes an elegant point—a poignant lesson for poets. In it, Deucalion's ark does not settle upon Mount Ararat, as Noah's did. Rather, as the waters recede, it nestles into a notch between two great mountains. When the ground has dried, Deucalion and company climb out, and it is no coincidence that they set their feet upon both Mount Parnassus—the home of the Muses of poetry and music—and the mountain of Bacchus—the god of revelry, theater, and wine (remember, even Noah planted a vineyard after he landed). Twin peaks. Poetry and celebration—both in response to the miracle of life.

Our creativity is the continuation of something that has been going on since the creation of the universe, and something that will continue to go on for a long time. We are, in a sense, part of a cosmic miracle, an eternal unfolding.

Being here, being one-in-80-billion and riding the Big Kahuna of Creation itself, is worth celebrating.

Exercises

- Go outside and notice everything around you. Are you able to be amazed—mystified—by what you see? Contemplate the objects you see until you begin to sense something strange and alien about them, until you realize that you never really knew them at all. That's the point at which you can start trying to communicate that feeling to others.

- English-American poet W. H. Auden (1907–1973) was fascinated by the magazine *Scientific American*. Although he said he often didn't understand the articles, the magazine helped him expand his vocabulary. He loved learning new words, their sounds and nuances. This week, pick up a copy of *Discover* magazine or some other science magazine and read a few articles about recent advances in science, especially astrophysics and atomic theory. Open your mind to the way scientists view the world.
- *Poem assignment.* One of the most anthologized poems by American poet Archibald MacLeish (1892–1982) is "Epistle to Be Left in the Earth." It is a somber poem, a letter the poet writes for some alien civilization to find long after humans have disappeared. In it, he lists whatever he thinks those aliens might want to know about us. Write a poem in which you itemize what you would want an alien civilization to know about us millions of years from now, perhaps long after all human life has vanished.

Reading

Helpful Resources

- Two small books that are accessible and enlightening about what's happening in modern science are *Star Talk* host Neil deGrasse Tyson's *Astrophysics for People in a Hurry* (2017) and Carlo Rovelli's international bestseller, *Seven Brief Lessons on Physics* (2014). Let yourself be amazed.
- For down-to-earth creativity and recycling what already exists, Austin Kleon's popular and viral little book, *Steal Like an Artist: 10 Things Nobody Told You about Being Creative* (2012) is tremendously enjoyable and wise.

- A good general guide to poetry writing and creativity is *The Poet's Companion: A Guide to the Pleasures of Writing Poetry* (1997).

Classic Poet

- One classic poet who has a sense of the cosmic nature of creativity is English poet and artist William Blake (1757–1827). If you've never read his poetry, start with *Songs of Innocence and of Experience*. It is mandatory reading, available in countless editions and online—though read them in facsimile editions accompanied by his own illustrations.

Contemporary Poet

- Utah poet-laureate David Lee (b. 1944), sometimes called "the porcine poet," has created a marvelous rural world out of Southern and Western culture, with a unique voice all his own. I recommend his volume *News from Down to the Café* (1999).

Part Two: Unearthing Poems

Poetry is a mystic, sensuous mathematics of fire, smoke-stacks, waffles, pansies, people, and purple sunsets.

—Carl Sandburg[1]

6

Imagery and the Senses: The Things of This World

From the outer edges of the universe, we now turn back to Planet Earth, in all its variety and minute detail; from the stars above our heads we turn to the soil beneath our feet.

While a poem must begin with an inkling of an idea, an off-the-wall notion, an emotion aching to be expressed, a word, a seed, it can only grow by being nourished, not just by what's in our head but by what's all around us. A poem comes to life for the reader when the poet's senses are engaged.

The Eyes of the Soul

In October 1893, a teenager wrote the following lines as part of a longer free-verse poem called "Autumn."

> But now a change o'er the bright and glorious sky has come
> The threatening clouds stand still,
> The silent skies are dark and solemn;
> The mists of morning hide the golden face of day.
> And a mysterious hand has stripped the trees;

And with rustle and whir the leaves descend,
And like little frightened birds
Lie trembling on the ground.

Walt Whitman it is not. The description is conventional, full of Victorian sentimentality. And yet, it's one the most remarkable poems ever written, for it was created by a thirteen-year-old girl who, since infancy, had been both blind and deaf. The poem was written by the young Helen Keller (1880–1968), who grew up to be a beloved writer, political activist, and mystic.[2]

How was it possible for her to envision autumn? Through what filter was she able to comprehend such common objects as trees and leaves and birds? What kind of imaginative leap made it possible for her to hear the nuances of *rustle* and *whir*?

Perhaps you've tried this old challenge—to describe a spiral without using your hands. It's not easy. What Helen Keller's teacher, Anne Sullivan, undertook was far more difficult—to describe an entire world to a young girl who lacked the two most essential of her five senses. Sullivan, who had herself gone partially blind at the age of five, accomplished this task in part by leading Keller, step-by-step, hand-in-hand, through the autumn woods of Massachusetts.

Many of the images in the poem are drawn from objects the poet could hold in her hands: rocks, leaves, snow, ice. Imagine how different sunlight and mist must seem to someone who feels them against her face instead of seeing what they look like. Keller learned the world through touch.

Somehow Sullivan even managed to explain colors. Elsewhere in the poem Keller refers to "the golden corn," "the golds, scarlets and purples" of the leaves, the "wild grapes, purple and fair and full of sunshine," the snowy "white and silent world." How does a person without sight imagine colors? Keller explained in a letter to a friend that the poem was "a word picture of Autumn as I see it with the eyes of my soul."[3]

Though the challenges Keller faced were great, she knew what poets have known since the beginning of time: poetry doesn't just speak the language of words, it speaks the language of the senses.

Things of This World

The common college-English term for this is *poetic imagery*; that is, using common objects, both for what they evoke in themselves and for their metaphorical resonance. But the word *imagery* is too limiting, for we tend to think of *images* as whatever we see with our eyes. The kind of *imagery* that poets use involves all the senses. Perhaps a more appropriate term would be *poetic sensuality*, by which I don't mean "sexy"—at least, not necessarily (more about that in chapter 11, "Love and Sex"). I mean "appealing to the senses," writing so that readers see, hear, smell, taste, and feel what you're getting at, in a way that's alive, invigorating, and, yes, even arousing. This is one of the first lessons taught in any creative-writing class.

In one of his most beautiful poems, the late American poet Richard Wilbur (1921–2017) recounts a morning on which he awoke, looked out the window to see laundry drying on a clothesline, and felt that "the morning air was all awash with angels." The poem is titled, "Love Calls Us to the Things of This World."[4]

That is a perfect description of the poet's calling. Love, which is Wilbur's word for that holy presence, doesn't call us to things we can't see, to spiritual concepts, gnostic theories, abstract notions. It doesn't call us to convey wise sentiments, teach deep lessons, or verbalize religious truths—who among us is arrogant enough to believe we are the possessors of such truths? Rather, Love calls us to experience the world in all its richness and sensuality, especially the minutiae that are seldom noticed, that are so common we hardly even see them anymore (… like the half moon at the base of your thumbnail, the smell of iron rusting in rain, the fact that different kinds of trees sound differently in the wind, the creamy softness of an older aunt's hand ...), and to experience them with no sermonizing or pedantry. Love calls us to give words to reality.

Exercises for the Senses

An entire genre of poetry exists that specializes in just this kind of sensual observation of the outer world: haiku. The form flourished in Japan in the seventeenth century, due to the acknowledged master of the form, Matsuo Basho (1644–1694). Most readers in the West remember him for this single haiku:

> An old pond
> a frog leaps in
> splash[5]

It may seem insubstantial, negligible even, but entire books have been written about just this one short poem. Learning the discipline of haiku can teach you a lot about the world, the senses, and about yourself.

The traditional rules of haiku are simple:

1. A haiku is arranged in three lines, the first having five syllables, the second seven, and the third five. (In the original Japanese, Basho's frog haiku does just that.)
2. A haiku contains a sensual, "seasonal image" (*kigo* in Japanese) that is, a reference to something in nature that evokes a specific time of year. Daffodils, for instance, conjure early spring; a dried maple leaf suggests autumn. Basho's frog is an image of summer.
3. A traditional Japanese haiku contains what's called a "cutting word" (*kireji*). This word can serve different functions depending on where in the haiku it is placed. For instance, when placed at the end, like the "splash" in Basho's haiku, it can serve as a kind of exclamation point. Sometimes, when used in the middle of the

poem, it marks the separation between two juxtaposed images, leaving readers to make the connection for themselves.

But listing such rules misses the point. The heart of the haiku is to open oneself to the world, to awaken the senses, to look outward without ego or agenda, to capture a single present moment and cherish it. Because of that, writing haiku can be a good way to practice poetry. It gets you into shape—like doing creative calisthenics. And insofar as every poem is "an act of gratitude," as Billy Collins said in chapter 3, writing haiku is a sort of spiritual calisthenics as well.

So Try This

Try writing one haiku (more if you can) every day for at least two weeks—better yet, for a month. Writing an entire poem a day is often beyond our capability, but most people can muster a haiku every twenty-four hours. With haiku, the pressure to be profound or wise or "poetic" has been removed; all you need is to note what you experience—and to make a small record of it.

Don't worry about "the rules." In fact, don't adhere to the seventeen-syllable rule at all; writers in English, because of the nature of our language, are able to cram far more detail into seventeen syllables than Japanese writers can. Instead, just make sure that each line has fewer than five/seven/five syllables (like the English translation of Basho's haiku above). That will come closer to simulating what Japanese poets do. And though I still cling to a seasonal word in every haiku (we can all use *some* discipline), many English writers don't bother with a "cutting word." It's up to you.

More importantly, get outside, take a walk down the street or into the woods, and be aware of what your senses experience. Don't think so much as feel, and then make a haiku. Day by day, record them in a notebook or on your phone or tablet.

One important rule is this: try *not* to make yourself the center of the experience, but expand your perceptions outward, and see yourself as an incredibly minor player in the scene all around you. Don't make the mistake that many poets in our individualistic Western culture make when they write haiku; that is, they use the form to display how clever or sensitive they are, as a way to show off. Rather, slip your ego into your pocket for a moment and just be. Nothing fogs up the windows of perceptions more quickly than an overblown sense of self. As Buddhist mindfulness teacher Sylvia Boorstein puts it in the title of her popular book, "Don't just do something. Sit there."

At first, you may feel that your little poems are inconsequential, like pennies that no one wants. But as a grade-school friend of mine once said, if you have a hundred thousand pennies, then you've got a thousand dollars. Practicing haiku every day is not unlike a teenage tennis player hitting a ball against the garage door. No single volley is important, but the cumulative effect is monumental.

At the end of the month, look back at what you've written. You may be surprised by how many of those haiku ideas and images can be used as seeds for other, longer poems at some point.

In and Through Nature

There is a spiritual dimension to all this. It's not just about objects. For the religious poet, "things"—especially the "things" of nature that are part of the divinely created order—have a special fascination, a profound resonance. English Romantic poet Samuel Taylor Coleridge (1772–1834) said that he found a "meditative joy" and "religious meanings in the forms of Nature!" In the poetry of the ancient Greeks, Coleridge felt, "all natural objects were *dead*, mere hollow statues. … [But] in the Hebrew poets each thing has a life of its own and yet they are all one life; in God they move and live and *have* their being; not *had*, as the cold system of Newtonian Theology represents, but *have*."[7]

Modern Nicaraguan poet, priest, and revolutionary Ernesto Cardenal (b. 1925), once put it this way: "What, after all, *are* things?" and he answered his own question, "They are God's love turned into things." He continued,

> God communicates with us by way of all things. They are messages and messengers of His love. When I am reading a book, it is He who speaks to me through its pages. I raise my eyes to look at a landscape, and I realize that it is God who has created this landscape, so that I should see it. And it was God who has inspired the artist to paint the picture at which I looked today, so that I should see it.[8]

For Coleridge and Cardenal, like Keller, it's about being aware of the vibrant spirit moving through the world, and, even more importantly, you are aware of being aware, noticing what you notice. Neuroscientists tell us that this sort of consciousness finds its source in the neocortex portion of our brain, the outermost layer that specializes in vision and hearing, and also the part that gives us our uniquely human ability to observe ourselves observing. Ask yourself, over and over again: *Why* did I especially notice (or remember or experience) that and not some other thing, and why is it important? What is God, speaking through the world, trying to say to me? If you can ask those questions, a poem is not far behind.

Out of Silence

We've discussed the inner silence of contemplative prayer already, but imagine what kind of inner silence Helen Keller must have experienced, and yet she was able to describe with great vividness the wonders of autumn—as well as so much else in the course of her writing.

Our journey, like hers, is from silence to "the things of this world," a process that is not about ourselves, but about paying attention in such a way as to forget ourselves in order to see clearly, to merge in some small way with what we are observing. Dwelling within that experience restores us, even if briefly, to our original place—an Edenic place—within the created order, not apart from it. The silence is a meeting place. Quiet, empty, naked, we stand in God's presence, having come through the doorway of observable "things."

Of course, it is God who has drawn us through that door, not we ourselves. Though God has always known us in our "inmost parts,"[9] it is only when we are still and listen—and touch and taste and see and feel—that we become aware of our own being known.

Exercises

- Wherever you are sitting right now—whether lying in bed, in your chair, or wherever—tally what each of your senses is experiencing right now. Gather it all in. What do you see, smell, touch, taste, and feel?
- *Poem exercise 1:* As described in this chapter, try writing a haiku every day for a month.
- *Poem exercise 2:* Write a poem describing a color without ever naming the color. Use objects instead. To make it more interesting, try doing what Anne Sullivan did: describe a color to someone who has not been able to see since birth. All the other senses may be used, but no visual imagery is allowed.

Reading

Helpful Resources

- A good book on getting out into nature and opening the senses is naturalist Tristan Gooley's *How to Read*

Nature: Awaken Your Senses to the Outdoors You've Never Noticed (2017).

- For an outstanding book on using your senses more in your writing, see Laura Deutsch's *Writing from the Senses: 59 Exercises to Ignite Creativity and Revitalize Your Writing* (2014).
- Few writers are able to coach you through that small step from contemplation to putting words on paper better than Clark Strand in his excellent book *Seeds from a Birch Tree: Writing Haiku as a Spiritual Journey* (1998).

Classic Poets

- For haiku, a good anthology is *The Essential Haiku: Versions of Basho, Buson, and Issa* (1995), edited by American poet Robert Hass (b. 1941). Also highly recommended is *The Narrow Road to the Deep North and Other Travel Sketches* by Matsuo Basho (1644–1694). Basho traveled Japan extensively on foot and recorded his experiences in mix of haiku and explanatory prose—called *haibun*. The book is a wonderful opportunity to look into a great artist's creative process.
- Chilean poet Pablo Neruda (1904–1973) wrote an entire set of poems called *Odes to Common Things* (1994, trans. Ken Krabbenhoft), in which he does exactly what we've outlined in this chapter: he examines in detail ordinary, everyday things and finds within them depth and joy and resonance. A delightful collection.

Contemporary Poet

- For themes of nature, activism, and the environment, I recommend most anything by Gary Snyder (b. 1930):

Riprap and Cold Mountain Poems (2009) is a classic. Also: *This Present Moment: New Poems* (2015). Snyder's *Turtle Island* (New Directions, 1974) was awarded a Pulitzer Prize, and his collection of essays *Practice of the Wild* (2010) is one of the best books ever written about our place in the natural world.

Poetry, noun: A species of magic.
—Rachel Tzvia Back[1]

7

Magic and Imagination: The Muses of Enchantment

We think of writers of fantasy fiction, like J. R. R. Tolkien and J. K. Rowling, as having exceptional imaginations, being able, as they are, to create entire worlds that convince us of their reality. They invent characters and places and even languages, and they bring them to life. They perform, in a small way, a godlike role, acting as creators and shapers of their own invented universes, which must be a bit of what it means to be made "in the image of God." Our species comes by its creativity honestly, this inherited urge to say, "Let there be ..."

But you too, as a writer of poems, create worlds every bit as much as the fiction writer does—a fresh imaginative world within every poem you write. The meaning of the Greek word for poet means "maker." You are a maker of worlds and a fabricator of new realities. Those worlds may be smaller—micro worlds—and often less epic, less dramatic than the novelists' worlds (though don't say that to poets like Homer, Ovid, Dante, Chaucer, Milton, or Blake, among countless others, whose poetic worlds are as rich as anything created by the greatest fantasy writers). The worlds inside your poems may be less elaborate, say, than Narnia or Middle Earth, but at their heart they are every bit as complex. Your job is to convince the reader.

From the idea of *images*, which we discussed in the previous chapter, it is but a small step to the *imagination*, which is the effective accumulation of persuasive images. That process of making our inner world real to the reader is what the literary scholars call *mimesis*, the imitation of reality, and the imagination is the key. This *mimesis* begins, of course, with our firm conviction in the reality of what we are writing about—we have to believe it with all our senses and with all our heart.

English poet William Blake (1757–1827) once wrote that his "great task" as a poet was

> To open the Eternal Worlds, to open the immortal Eyes
> Of Man inwards into the Worlds of Thought: into Eternity
> Ever expanding in the Bosom of God, the Human
>   Imagination ...[2]

It's a startling declaration—to suggest that our creativity somehow lives within the very heart of God, that God intended us to be vibrant, imaginative beings.

Different kinds of imagination exist: the scientific, which plays creatively with facts and data; the philosophic, which squeezes truths out of abstractions. And various kinds of artistic imagination exist: the theatrical, the musical, the pictorial, and so on.

As far as the poetic imagination, I believe it involves something unexpected, perhaps even shocking at its core, because poets have one formidable advantage over scientists or philosophers or musicians when it comes to the imaginative realm: poetry is rooted in magic. In other words, there is something otherworldly in the process by which we make our world real to the reader.

Enchantment

First, a disclaimer: I'm as thoroughgoing a skeptic as you're likely to meet. When it comes to ghosts, conjurers, UFOs, the occult, Big Foot, Nostradamus, and other such phenomena, whether New Age or age old, I'm a cynic.

But unlike some people who dismiss the paranormal out of hand and feel obliged to disabuse the True Believers of their faith, I have a different response. For me, my skepticism is like an immunization shot that allows me to travel, healthy and unharmed, through those exotic lands, be they supernatural or superstitious—without catching the local diseases. In many ways, I believe I enjoy those foreign places more than the actual inhabitants do because I can appreciate the tourist sites objectively, seeing them as imaginative possibilities rather than facts or dogmas. I can relish their mythopoeic grandeur without having to debate their reality.

Those useful mythologies contain a great number of cultural "things" that are every bit as useful—and every bit as *real*—to poems as the physical "things" that appeal to our senses. Even our most brilliant Christian fantasy writers like George MacDonald, C. S. Lewis, J. R. R. Tolkien, and J. K. Rowling relish those magic, mythic, and supernatural elements and use them—freely and liberally—in their works. And, truth be told, each of those writers was really a poet at heart.

Poetry and Magic

So I repeat, poetry is rooted in magic. Old magic. Primordial. Among the earliest civilizations, it was the exalted language reserved for invoking the gods, blessing the harvests, cursing one's enemies, recounting the exploits of heroes. It was the language of priests; both the Sibylline and Delphic oracles spoke their cryptic, mysterious prophecies in verse. For ordinary people, poems existed to expel bad spirits, overcome illness, cast a love charm—and they were often recited in combination with making ritual gestures and lighting fires, casting sticks, or offering sacrifices.

Poetry was then (and just below the surface remains) a form of incantation—a midpoint between superstition and prayer. It is the most potent form of communication developed by humans, one that spans nearly all languages, and the old magic, I believe, is like an electric hum that vibrates at low volume, just below the level of auditory awareness, whenever we create poems. We no longer cast spells, summon spirits, or call down curses, though there are poems that do that (like "Traveller's Curse after Misdirection" by Robert Graves [1895–1985]). Poetry is not magic in the way that it used to be. But in another sense, we do those things implicitly when we write poetry because we can't escape its inherent incantatory power.

The root of the word *incantation* goes back to the Latin *incantare*—"to enchant"—which itself is rooted in the word *cantare,* "to sing." Ancient "singers" were both poets and enchanters. It is said that Homer (seventh century BCE) not only sang *The Iliad* and *The Odyssey*, the great hero tales of Greek myth, but in his ability to "conjure" those worlds to life, he was thought of as an enchanter as well.

To enchant was to sing in such a way as to bring people and objects—even nature itself—within the range of one's will. In Greek mythology, for instance, the forest trees would bend achingly toward legendary poet and musician Orpheus as he sang, and the city of Thebes virtually leaped into existence when Amphion, son of Zeus, sang to the accompaniment of his golden lyre.

In our ancient English ballads, which are full of enchanted songs and singers, the man who stole the heart of the Fairy Queen was named not just Thomas, an ordinary enough name, but Thomas *the Rhymer*. And the familiar "parsley, sage, rosemary, and thyme" of the English folksong "Scarborough Fair" are not just good herbs in a stew; they are a love potion, a charm, so that "then she'll be a true love of mine."

Poetic incantation is so common that we pay it little attention to it. For instance,

He loves me.
He loves me not.
He loves me.
He loves me not.
He loves me.

Accompanied by the plucking of flower petals, it is a spoken and enacted ritual that has been performed, even if whimsically, for centuries. The first characteristic of such incantation is that it evokes nature—in this case a flower. Poetry, as we've said before, traffics in created things.

Structurally, "He loves me" is pure repetition, which is the second attribute of incantation. The repeated lines are, paradoxically, both soporific and emphatic, having the power to lull as well as focus one's attention. The words build suspense, and each time they are repeated, the lover is reminded that the outcome hangs in the balance.

Third, this incantation seeks to bend fate to one's will. It has the effect of a spell, incorporating not only the lover's own desire but the force of nature itself in convincing the loved one to return the love.

Fourth, notice the power of the rhythm. The first line ends in a trochee (two stressed syllables: "he *loves me*"); the second line is a pair of iambs ("he *loves me not*"). What is so fascinating about this rhythm is that the hoped-for outcome ("he loves me") is the stronger, more potent phrase. The second line is a bit weaker by comparison, because that is not the result the lover wishes.

Consider another example:

Star light, star bright,
First star I see tonight;
I wish I may, I wish I might
Have the wish I wish tonight.

Note that the same elements: the invocation of nature, the repetitions, the yearning to effect change, and the powerful rhythm (I love the opening line with its four stressed syllables, followed by two stressed syllables at the beginning of the second line). Mysteriously, the wish itself remains unspoken, as though to speak it might diminish its chance of coming true (as in blowing out the candles on a birthday cake—another of our common rituals). This unspokenness reminds us that implication is often more powerful than explication; that is, we don't always need to say everything. It is the almost said.

Notice that "Star light, star bright" adds an element missing from "He loves me": Rhyme. (We'll talk more about that in chapter 12 on "Rhyme, Meter, and Forms.")

Beyond Pagan Incantation

If we're serious about poetry, we learn to exploit the kind of imaginative enchantment that it entails, a magic that is at once potent and yet safe enough for a child, a magic that seems to subvert traditional faith but actually enlivens and strengthens it. Lest we think it is superstitious drivel, we need only turn to the Psalms to find these same incantatory elements: nature, repetition, the hope of changing outcomes, and powerful rhythms. Consider these imprecatory (cursing) lines from Psalm 35, in which the psalmist asks the Lord to defeat his enemies:

> Let them be confounded and put to shame that seek after my soul: let them be turned back and brought to confusion that devise my hurt. Let them be as chaff before the wind: and let the angel of the Lord chase them. Let their way be dark and slippery: and let the angel of the Lord persecute them. For without cause have they hid for me their net in a pit, which without cause they have digged for my soul.

Wow! Just wow!

Or consider the following traditional Celtic Christian incantation from among many collected by the great folklorist Alexander Carmichael (1832–1912) in remote parts of Scotland. If you are familiar with the poetry of William Butler Yeats (1865–1939), Padraic Colum (1881–1972), George Mackay Brown (1921–1996), and other Irish and Scottish poets, then you'll see where they get their incantatory power from. Instead of a curse, these lines offer a blessing, which is a sort of charm:

> Since Thou Christ it was who didst buy the soul—
> At the time of yielding the life,
> At the time of pouring the sweat,
> At the time of offering the clay,
> At the time of shedding the blood,
> At the time of balancing the beam,
> At the time of severing the breath,
> At the time of delivering the judgment,
> Be its peace upon Thine own ingathering;
> Jesus Christ Son of gentle Mary,
> Be its peace upon Thine own ingathering,
> O Jesus! upon Thine own ingathering.

This poem is filled with stunning phrases, such as describing the death of Jesus as his "ingathering" and the "severing" of his breath, and it shows just how incantation crosses over into prayer. Notice the rhythms and the repetition. It is an Easter hymn of extraordinary power.

Why Is Magic Important?

What do incantation—and the enchantment it evokes—have to do with writing poetry in the twenty-first century? Does poetry change anything? Does it conjure magic? Does a harvest blessing bring better crops? Can poetry defeat our enemies?

No, of course not. But also … yes.

The fact is, the harvest does come. In early times, if it was plentiful, the ancient priest would have attributed it to the power of the incantation. If the harvest was disappointing, then perhaps the formula wasn't potent enough, in which case it will be improved the following year.

But the real power of incantation, and of poetry in general, is not how it changes the outer world but how it changes the inner one—the writer's own created world. You can see that in the Celtic prayer. The agony Christ experienced in his "ingathering" is the source of the soul's peace—for he "didst buy the soul." It is a powerful transformation, from cruel death to blessed peace, which is even more monumental than the most abundant harvest.

This transformation is why, as Billy Collins said, we turn to poetry in times of crisis and upheaval. We hope that by saying just the right words, we can undo devastation, raise the dead, grant second chances, dissuade events from ever happening in the first place, or just experience a bit of distance from or power over our situation. In the interior country of poetic imagination, as with God, all things are possible.

Our words will not change the world. But as we unwrap our experiences, and the difficult emotions that are embedded within them, in the form of poems, we succeed in changing our hearts, and, we hope, the reader's. We find a different perspective. A more realistic one. We find the beginnings of healing. And hope. Which is why we write.

How many news broadcasts have you sat through that just chatter in the dark? How many words, words, words do people fling about every day, talking and talking (as I'm doing now)—like heaving clods of dirt to remove a boulder in the path—when just few words of magic would suffice?

Poetry is that place where a few well-chosen words suffice. In times like ours, we are called to put aside the many words and take up the few. We may not be enchanters like Merlin or Gandalf, but we are the enchanters of our own souls. Our goal is to enchant our readers' souls as well.

Exercises

- Read some poems from your favorite anthology, and look for the incantatory elements: the invoking of nature, repetition, strong rhythms and rhyme, the desire to change the world both externally and internally.
- Now, do the same for the poems you have written, paying attention to any changes that take place within them, the desires and yearnings, the magic you hoped to impose on your inner world. Although the world may not have changed because of your poems, to what extent has your attitude toward the world changed?
- *Poem assignment:* Write an intentionally incantatory poem, either a charm or a curse or a blessing, using the repetitive list format seen in the Celtic prayer.

Reading

Helpful Resources

- Already recommended in chapter 3 ("Silence—The Infinite Longing"), Robert McDowell's *Poetry as a Spiritual Practice: Reading, Writing, and Using Poetry in Your Daily Rituals, Aspirations, and Intentions* (2008) is worth looking into.
- I also highly recommend Esther de Waal's *The Celtic Way of Prayer: The Recovery of the Religious Imagination* (Image, 1999), in which she explains the beauty and power of Celtic prayers and hymns.

Classic Poets

- De Waal has also edited a selection from Alexander Carmichael's *Carmina Gadelica* in a book called *The Celtic Vision: Prayers, Blessings, Songs, and Invocations from the Gaelic Tradition* (2001).
- Charles Causley (1917–2003) was a poet from Cornwall, England, who was immersed in folklore traditions. He edited *The Puffin Book of Magic Verse* (Puffin, 1974), a delightful collection of charms, nursery rhymes, and dozens of poems from such classic English poets as Shakespeare, Keats, Yeats, and Frost.

Contemporary Poets

- One poet who immediately comes to mind when talking about changing our inner world is Sebastian Matthews (b. 1965) in his book *Beginner's Guide to a Head-On Collision* (2017). It is a memoir in poems, about his recovery from a near-fatal car-accident in which his wife and son were also involved. It is powerful, often humorous, and moving.
- Somewhat lighter but powerful nonetheless is the book of children's poems by poet Joyce Sidman (b. 1956), *What the Heart Knows: Chants, Charms, and Blessings* (Houghton Mifflin Harcourt, 2013), stunningly illustrated by Pamela Zagarenski

The Land of Dreams is better far
Above the light of the Morning
Star.

—William Blake[1]

8

Intuition and Dreams: The Back Roads of the Brain

Were I a student at Hogwarts, I would ask Hermione Granger to find a spell that would allow me to conjure instant, startling verbal connections, stunning images of the kind that would make my poems compelling, insightful, and memorable … like the great poets do. In my mind, it's the only spell worth having.

What I want is the kind of wizardry Medieval French poet François Villon (1431–c. 1463) practiced when he described the frigid winter of 1456 as "the dead season / when the wolves lived on wind."[2] Or when Emily Dickinson (1830–1886) called the noise a fly makes a "Blue—uncertain stumbling Buzz."[3] Or when Rita Dove (b. 1952) described the taste of chocolate as "Knotted smoke, dark punch / of earth and night and leaf."[4]

These images take the common stuff of the world—wind, blue, smoke, night—and then serve it up fresh to the reader in the most astonishing ways. Making such magical, unexpected connections is, after all, what poets do. It is our métier. It's what

Elizabethan poet Sir Philip Sidney meant when he stated that poets "make the too much loved earth more lovely."[5] It's what English Romantic poet Percy Bysshe Shelley (1792–1822) was getting at when he wrote, "Poetry … awakens and enlarges the mind itself by rendering it the receptacle of a thousand unapprehended combinations of thought. Poetry lifts the veil from the hidden beauty of the world, and makes familiar objects be as if they were not familiar."[6]

Unlearning

So how do we make the familiar *un*familiar?

The answer is by doing it, though it is something each poet must learn by himself or herself "in the still night," as Dylan Thomas says, "when only the moon rages."[7] As with finding our personal process, no one can do it for us.

Perhaps it is not so much about learning something new as it is about unlearning something old—letting go of the fusty, tired connections we've made for years and abandoning our conventional ways of looking at the world. For instance, Rita Dove doesn't describe chocolate with "tasty" adjectives like *luscious, sweet, pungent.* Instead, she draws her images from the senses of sight, smell, and touch. Likewise, in his poem, Villon doesn't call the winter *cold* or *snowy* or *frigid*; instead, he says it's the "dead season," and then, in a masterstroke, he gives us those hungry, wind-devouring wolves. It's chilling in more ways than one.

Of course, we needn't feel obliged to shoehorn those kinds of stunning, spectacular images into our poems. They are not for everyone or for every poem. Artificiality is not good. Many poets shun such imagistic pyrotechnics and write in a more direct, unadorned way; many poets who take nature as their major theme come to mind, people like Gary Snyder (b. 1930), Catherine Abbey Hodges (b. 1959), and Kathleen Jamie (b. 1962). In fact, when done too often, such sparkling images can start to look contrived, over-clever, or self-indulgent.

Still, being able to come up with one or two of them when needed is a useful tool to have in the toolbox. So how do we *unlearn* to do that?

Intuition

To perform that kind of magic, the rational mind, the intellect, is not the best place to start. Rather, we have to depend on intuition, which, try as I might through the years, I've found can't be commanded and made to jump through hoops like a circus dog. The funniest people I've known tell me that they come up with their most brilliant comic quips not by thinking about them but by letting them sort of emerge out of the inner mist of the mind. Their humor is spontaneous. And the same, perhaps, is true for brilliant poetic images.

If you are someone who already has that kind of immediate intuition, consider yourself blessed. But even those who have that gift in abundance sometimes find it helpful to resort to techniques that have been proven to help spark those kinds of connections.

One place to explore is free-associative writing, described in chapter 4 ("Process: The Empty Page"). By allowing the imagination to run wild, jotting down whatever occurs to us, steam-of-consciousness-style, we can let the unconscious mind take the lead. It's a sort of a verbal Rorschach test. You write what comes to mind and you move on to the next thing that comes to mind. Eventually, you get in the habit of zigging when your conscious brain wants to zag. At times, you hit upon interesting connections, the best of which can be saved and used in poems. Certain risks come with this kind of writing, which can produce vast expanses of useless drivel, but every so often you find disparate ideas that connect in an interesting way. Twice I've experienced whole, finished poems emerging, with no revisions needed, from such rapid, free writing.

Another technique is synesthesia, that is, focusing on an awareness of how your physical sensations overlap, flowing into one another so that sounds, for instance, are allowed to have color and certain smells are free to evoke places and objects. In the samples above, Emily Dickinson—one of the world's great synesthetic poets—thinks of the fly's buzzing as blue, and Rita Dove associates the taste of chocolate with the smell of smoke.

The most famous practitioner of poetic synesthesia was French symbolist Arthur Rimbaud (1854–1891), who wrote some of the world's most remarkable poems before giving up writing at the age of twenty-one. In a letter to a friend, written in 1871 when Rimbaud was sixteen, he declared that "the poet becomes a seer through the long, immense, deliberate disordering of all the senses."[8] For example, his famous poem "Voyelles" ("Vowels") associates each vowel in the alphabet with entire worlds of sensual experience; for him, the letter *I* evokes "purples, spit blood, laughter of beautiful lips / in anger or penitent drunkenness."[9]

So, as you write, be conscious of your sensual perceptions, and don't assume that everything you can see must have a visual adjective in front of it. Verbs of taste do not need to have nouns of taste as their subject or object. Challenge yourself to find olfactory words to describe tactile experiences, or tactile words to describe auditory experiences, and so on.

Follow Your Dreams

When I was reading Rimbaud in my teens, I knew that my natural synesthetic skills were limited. Later I wrote a poem called "Reply to Rimbaud" in which I describe the mysterious emptiness that is, for me, at the heart of each of the vowels. It began:

> I do not claim to know what vowels convey.
> They are inscrutable. Their mystery
> is that of ciphers. Blank geometry.
> A map of water. Duller than the day
> that came before my earliest memory.[10]

But at about the same age, I managed to find another back road to the unconscious mind: the path of dreams.

The "dream poem" is an age-old literary device used to justify all sorts of curious unconventionality. It was popular in the Middle Ages: "Piers Plowman," "The Dream of the Rood," Chaucer's "Parlement of Foules," "The Romance of the Rose," and many others all pretend to be dream visions. The coy game is that both the author and the reader know they're not.

But that's not what I'm talking about. Rather, I'm interested in those nexuses between our nighttime dreams—medieval mystics and the Romantic poets alike would have considered them "visions"—and our creativity, the blue highways in and out of our unconscious minds. An English professor once told me, "If you want to write poetry, you have to eat, breathe, and sleep poetry."[11] I've come to realize that the part about "sleeping poetry" was not hyperbolic. Sleep is one of our best stimulants to the poetic process.

I have this fanciful notion that the Muses park their RVs in our unconscious brains, and while we sleep, they climb out, string up the paper lanterns, pour the mai tais, and party all night. And they also party in that half-sleeping, half-waking state for which we don't have a good word in English (though I think it's akin to what is sometimes called lucid dreaming). You've had that experience of dreaming that you're falling and you wake up with a jolt just before hitting the ground. It's that place … where strange, evanescent notions come to you, where divergent, absurd ideas make fascinating connections, where the barrel teeters on the edge of Niagara. Almost as soon as you wake, the connection evaporates. But sometimes you can catch them before they vanish.

In sleep, the mind offers us images, ideas, notions, people, sounds, bits of stories, sensations—and sometimes even words. Poet Lawrence Ferlinghetti wrote, "Poetry is news from the growing edge on the far frontiers of consciousness."[12] Most poets draw from their dreams, and often, the more irrational the dreams are, the more intriguing. They remind us that what is suggested is as important as what is said. Dreams are, in a sense, suggestiveness in its purest form.

The trick is in making this kind of awareness part of your poetic process. Try inviting all those crazy notions that inhabit your sleep to make their way into your poems—all those images, scenes, characters, feelings, transformations, confusions, and so on. They are the stuff of your inner world every bit as much as trees and laundry hanging dry and chocolate are the stuff of your outer world. Your brain is whispering to you, and you should listen.

Travel Tips for Those Back Roads

Here are few guidelines for letting those horses of the unconscious mind out of the stable:

- First, *write it down.* Whether you have a crazy dream or just an odd, half-conscious thought while waiting for an elevator, write it down immediately. Otherwise, you'll forget it. Make it a habit to never be without your notebook or a slip of paper by your bedside and in your pocket. At your local office-supply store, you can purchase special pens that light up as you write, making it easy to record your dreams at night without getting out of bed and turning on the light. The important thing is not to lose those transitory thoughts.
- Second, *listen to the longing.* As we grow older, we often inure ourselves to the heartbreak, pain, and loss we've known in the past. Those pangs you experienced when a pet died forty years ago, when a romance died thirty years ago, or when a parent died just last month can come back to you in a dream. Be willing to revisit that pain. The fact is, that pain is demanding attention. So you need to listen to it.

- Third, *trust the bizarre.* Especially the bizarre. Learn to make a place setting for odd notions at your creative dinner table, and the let them tell you their story. Dreams are good at exposing the "taboos" and difficult emotions in your life, so pay attention to them. Even Freud said that the more uncomfortable it makes you, the more meaningful it is.
- Fourth, *approach dreams as if they are real* because, in a sense, they are. That is, if you dream about swimming across the Amazon River on your back, there is no law that says you can write about that is if it really happened. If you find yourself dreaming about being lost in endless, winding corridors (a common dream for me), write about that experience. It *is* your experience after all. No need to apologize or explain.
- Finally, *make it interesting.* Remember the reader. Your symbols aren't always the reader's, so find a common language and touch something human. Toss your random dream images and longings into the paint box and squeeze out their color when it's appropriate. Remember: poetry is about your relationship with the reader.

So give it a try. Next time you're strapped for subjects, take a nap. But keep a pen handy and one eye open for dreams.

A Footnote to Dreams

One final note: I'm fascinated by the fact that we can sometimes—once in a great while—travel those blue highways in the other direction as well … not just when bits of dreams seep into our poetry but when bits of poetry seep into our dreams. English literature is full of examples.

In the late seventh century, a man named Caedmon worked as a farmhand at an English abbey. At special feasts, the monks and workers would "pass the harp" to entertain each other by singing improvised songs—the social media of the time. On these occasions, Caedmon would creep out to the barn before the harp was passed to him because, being illiterate, he was ashamed of having no talent for such displays. One night Caedmon had a powerful dream in which a mysterious figure told him to sing about "the beginning of created things." In the dream, Caedmon composed the beginning of a poem, now called "Caedmon's Hymn," part of which is given here:[13]

> Now should we praise of the kingdom of heaven the Warden,
> Of the Creator the might, and his mind-thought [purpose],
> the work of the Gloryfather, just as he of wonders,
> eternal Lord, created the beginning [of each].
> He first created for the children of earth
> heaven as a roof, holy Shaper;
> then Middle Earth mankind's Warden,
> eternal Lord, after created
> for men the earth, Ruler almighty.[14]

Another example: in the summer of 1797, Samuel Taylor Coleridge (1772–1834) fell asleep (opium-induced) and dreamed the beginning of a poem called "Kubla Khan." Such was the brilliance of his mind that when he awoke, he could remember, he said, every one of the two-to-three-hundred lines he had dreamed. Then, as fate would have it, before he'd transcribed even half the poem to paper, a "person from Porlock" knocked at the door and simultaneously knocked the poem right out of Coleridge's head.[15]

You may have read about "sleep learning." For decades, researchers have known that you can actually learn in your sleep, that if you think about memorizing French verb constructions as you're falling asleep, for instance, you have a better chance of retaining them. This same theory applies to your poetry—you can "sleep poetry," as my professor said. By thinking about your writing as you lie in bed, waiting for sleep to come, you increase your chances of not only learning more about the craft of poetry but also having poetry seep into your dreams.

I first experienced this kind of sleep learning years ago when I was reading one of the "prophetic" works of William Blake (1757–1827) just before bed. That night, I dreamed I had written a "Blakean" poem myself, though I could only remember one line upon waking: "The eel has pulled the eagle from his hole in the sky." Not bad, I thought, a bit like some of the lines from Blake's *Marriage of Heaven and Hell*, and I was intrigued enough to use it in a poem later.

Another time, while writing haiku in my head while coming in and out of sleep one hot August morning, these lines came in a dream:

You. I. Who are we?
The dust we raise on the path
settles soon enough.

The longest poem I ever wrote in a dream (and it was not opium-induced) is the following, which was written during a bout of jetlag after returning from a trip to China, while I was reading a lot of Han Shan, the legendary Chinese poet. Here is what I transcribed in my notebook, word for word, upon waking:

We sit quietly in the sun
shawls covering our laps
too old to remember our ages
and suddenly I have an idea
quick, someone—fold poems into little pills
and place them under our tongues
I've no idea what Shades
may dwell on the other side
but surely it will help to have
some poetry already on our lips

I later rewrote the poem with a different slant, and it was published.[16]

Big Sky Mind

Zen Buddhists have a concept they call "big sky mind." The big sky is the limitless, blank, blue sky, arching from one far horizon to the other, and it is a metaphor for the unconscious mind we're hardly aware of. It is the opposite of what is called "monkey mind," which is the constant, conscious, distracting chatter that goes on in our brains.

High above, almost invisible because of its distance, a single bird is soaring. It is our urge to write a poem, no more than a speck in the vast universe of possibilities. The bird has the entire sky in which to soar and glide.

As you drift off to sleep, let that bird soar in that huge blue sky. Then see what happens.

Exercises

- Look at Rita Dove's description of chocolate again. Think of a taste that appeals to you, and then describe it in evocative terms by using the *other* senses only.
- For one month, keep a dream journal. Many people say they never remember their dreams, but they often find that once they try keeping a dream journal, they become more conscious of them. After a month, see what kind fodder for poems the journal might offer.
- *Poem assignment:* make a list of five nouns, and then pair them with synesthetic adjectives or verbs. Now, fill in the gaps. Connect those word combinations in some creative way.

Reading

Helpful Resources

- For helping you with your writing, Natalie Goldberg's *Writing Down the Bones: Freeing the Writer Within* (2005) is unexcelled.

Classic Poets

- If you haven't read Coleridge's "Kubla Kahn" since high school, now's the time to revisit that remarkable poem. It's available online and in most any anthology of English poetry. While you're there, reread "Rhyme of the Ancient Mariner" as well.
- Though not necessarily inspired by actual dreams, the collected *Dream Songs* (1969) by American poet John Berryman (1914–1972) are intriguing, baffling, powerful, and most certainly dreamlike.

Contemporary Poets

- Most good poets are able to make startling, imaginative verbal connections. That's what they do. So, it is hard to name just a couple. Some younger poets who have caught my attention recently in that regard are Ocean Vuong's *Night Sky with Exit Wounds* (2016).
- American Pulitzer Prize–winning poet and former US poet laureate Kay Ryan (b. 1945) is especially good at capturing those micro-notions that seem to come from that half-sleep territory. Her 2015 collection *Erratic Facts* is especially enjoyable.

Expect nothing. Live frugally
on surprise.

—Alice Walker
(b. 1944)[1]

9

Insight and Surprise: One Hand Clapping

As we've said repeatedly, a poem grows out of an insight, a notion, a story, an observation, a long-suppressed emotion, a sudden awareness, or a combination of those—something the poet wants, needs, to communicate. Writing a poem is both a spiritual act and a relational one. When you give the poem to the reader, it should have nothing whatsoever to do with preaching or teaching, and everything to do with showing rather than telling, as every writing teacher will tell you. A poem is a map that outlines, step by step, how the writer arrived at that particular place. The key is to bring the reader along, to reach the point of discovery, together, in real time.

So how do we do that?

The Sound of One Hand

"Two hands clapping make a sound. What is the sound of one hand?"[2]

That, as you may know, is the most famous *koan* devised by Japanese Zen master Hakuin Ekaku (1686–1768), who was also a calligrapher, painter, and poet. In the practice of Zen, a koan is a statement or a question given to a student for the purpose of meditation, the point of which is to track the student's progress along their path toward enlightenment, the state of being awakened to the essential nature of reality.

When my daughters were young, I found myself immersed in short poetic forms, pentastichs, Sufi quatrains, and Zen haiku, because I was so busy. With small children, one has little time for long poems (or books in general, for that matter), but short poems can be wiggled into the schedule between diaper changes and 2:00 a.m. feedings.

When my middle daughter, Molly, was about four years old, I told her about Zen koans, and, thinking it would be fun to mystify her with a little Hakuin, I said, "He used to ask his students, 'What is the sound of one hand clapping?'"

"That's easy," said Molly. She showed me her right hand, then opened and closed it, smacking the fingers on the palm.

I was dumbfounded. She cut through the mystification and went straight to the obvious, the unaffected, the transparent. In all the years that I'd known about that famous koan, Molly's answer never occurred to me. Countless books have been written about Zen, delving into the mysteries of emptiness, relinquishment of self, mind without mind, the futility of intellectual striving, and so on—concepts too deep for me. But I suspect that Molly's answer never occurred to any of those writers either. I don't know if Hakuin would have declared her enlightened, but in a small way, I was.

I drew two lessons from that experience, the first of which is akin to what's known as "Occam's razor." Occam, a fourteenth-century English theologian, devised a rule for grappling with difficult concepts: Do not overcomplicate things unnecessarily—the simplest approach is the right one. Molly's hand clap was so simple as to undercut, in her child's way, volumes of arcane philosophy. A poem does the same thing. It says what's needed without overcomplicating it.

The second lesson is that as we write about our insights, our small enlightenments, they should take us, and the reader, by surprise in some small way. Our revelations are best when they are fresh, even never thought-of before. If we start a poem knowing what we expect to discover, then we haven't discovered anything at all. We're just narrating our premeditated talking points. We have to convey not just our thoughts about life, but a bit of our astonishment as well.

The trick is to allow ourselves to be surprised, which requires a certain amount of humility beforehand, a certain childlikeness, and a firm assumption that we don't know everything. Read any good poem, and you'll notice this: the poet isn't telling; the poet is exploring and taking you along for the ride.

Insights All Around

Small revelations, mini enlightenments, startling insights are always at hand, and they are much closer, nearer to the surface of life, than we realize. While we may call such phenomena serendipity or grace, epiphany or *wabi-sabi*, vision or intuition, they are everywhere, every moment; you just need to look for them.

Right now, as I write this, I gaze out my office window in the city where I work:

- evaporating jet trails in the morning sky look like Morse code.
- a maintenance man hauls a trash can to the Dumpster; his slow pace conveys a burden of weariness that speaks volumes.
- sunlight reflects off the month-old snow, but it still sparkles everywhere. This makes me think of the homeless man who once stopped me on the street in my hometown when I was a child. He pointed to the mica flecks in the sidewalk and said, "It looks like diamonds!"

- the windows of the office building opposite are warped, creating a surreal video of the cars and people passing; it makes me think of the line by French poet Charles Baudelaire (1821–1867): "Swarming city, city full of dreams / Where ghosts reach out and grab passersby in broad daylight."
- I can just make out the osprey nest clumped on the cell tower two blocks away; I gaze at it. I wait. I wonder if the osprey have wintered here.

These are unexpected and undeserved gifts that move us, even if only a little. The heart skips, and we're grateful to be alive. And they are seeds for poems, each and every one. As American poet James Tate (1943–2015) wrote, "Poetry is everywhere; it just needs editing."[4] It is important to look for those gifts, seeking out the wonder that make your heart skip.

Nature is one of the great teachers in this way. Step outside and walk. Sometimes at night, a meteor blazes for a moment and then fades like an afterimage. But in those few seconds, the heart seems to jump sideways. A snowy owl flies across the path in winter. A fish leaps out of the water just beside the boat. A streak of chain lightning noiselessly zigzags from west to east. These events root you in a moment of time, making every nerve stand at attention like uncoiling ferns. William Wordsworth (1770–1850) wrote, "My heart leaps up when I behold / A rainbow in the sky."

Consider this example from haiku poet Kobayashi Issa (1762–1828). In spite of his tragic life, he wrote some of the most delightful poems ever written, and he specialized in these kinds of insights. Here's one he wrote about that funny way dogs cock their heads when they look at you—but in Issa's imagination, it takes a different turn:

> The dog tilts its head—
> as if listening to
> the earthworms singing[5]

Another example: Welsh poet W. H. Davies (1871–1940) doesn't just describe bumble-bees, he makes them come alive for the reader:

> ... to my garden back I come,
> Where bumble-bees for hours and hours
> Sit on their soft, fat, velvet bums
>   To wriggle out of hollow flowers.[6]

That's what I want for my poetry: not just beauty or craftsmanship; not just sonority or insight, as important as those are. In fact, I can forgive most failings in a poem as long as one thing is present: genuine, thrilling, effervescent surprise. I want to hear that single unexpected hand clap. I want my poems, at least some of the time, to contain a little time bomb that either goes piff, or bang, or *kaboom*.

To surprise the reader, we have to surprise ourselves, even if that means blowing up the scheme we had in mind for a poem, especially when we feel the writing is coming too slowly or too methodically. We have to veer in a different direction.

Think of W. B. Yeats's poem "The Second Coming." After spending the first thirteen lines of the poem evoking images of chaos and anarchy, he shifts to the "rough beast," a horrifying creature, who stalks out of the Egyptian desert to create for the world an apocalyptic nightmare.[7] It's stunning and takes you off guard.

Childhood

All of these poets—Hakuin, Issa, Davies, Cocteau, Yeats—have one thing in common. At their best, they achieved that state of constant astonishment because they looked through a child's eyes. In the child's world, all things are new. Everything is an enlightenment because everything is lit from within—a *light-within-ment.*

Restoration cleric and poet Thomas Traherne wrote of his childhood:

> How like an angel came I down!
> How bright are all things here!
> When first among his works I did appear
> O how their glory me did crown!
> The world resembled his eternity,
> In which my soul did walk;
> And every thing that I did see
> Did with me talk.[8]

William Wordsworth came to a similar conclusion in his "Ode on Intimations of Immortality":

> There was a time when meadow, grove, and stream
> The earth, and every common sight
>   To me did seem
>   Appareled in celestial light,
> The glory and the freshness of a dream.[9]

Children have a knack for seeing plainly. With fresh eyes. They perceive that the world is still glowing from having been created in the first place—still warm from the forge of that fire, as I like to say. They don't know that thousands of meteors flash through the sky every night all over the world, so for them, a single meteor is a stupendous event. And what's more, they're not burdened with the scientific understanding of what meteors are. For children, meteors are special, like miracles. The key is seeing like children—seeing both plainly and through the naïveté of wonder. Why else would Jesus recommend that we become like little children? Because when they enter God's kingdom, which is the present moment, they see it with new eyes, clear eyes, simple eyes.

I love what Robert Graves once said in a lecture:

> We have narrowed our minds by a neglect of the physical senses: relying on reason, we no longer see, hear, taste, smell or feel anything like so acutely as our primitive

> ancestors did, or as most little children still do before their education hardens.[10]

As adults, we need to learn this kind of childlikeness. Here's a story to illustrate what I mean. Just last year, my wife and I went to our local Japanese garden to take in the blossoming cherry trees. As we rounded one corner, we greeted an older gentleman, who was seated on a stone bench. He was frail and had a walker beside him. He smiled at us and laughed, "All this beauty and I'm only looking at the moon!" Sure enough, a pale quarter moon could be seen in the sunny, late afternoon sky. It was a surprise, a haiku thought full of beauty and simplicity, a moment of enlightenment. Not one minute later, my wife and I ran into a friend of ours who is a widely published poet. He was excited because, inspired by the blooming cherries, he too had written a poem. It was only five lines, but it was dense and complicated, and I don't remember a single word of it. No need explaining which "poem" I was more impressed with or which one made my heart leap.

Earlier I used that metaphor of the heart skipping when we see a meteor and when Wordsworth saw a rainbow. I wonder if the heart isn't actually leaping *toward* the meteor and the rainbow. Like a center fielder vaulting high against the outfield wall to catch a fly ball, the heart is springing *toward* those moments of surprise, trying to catch them all in its mitt.

At a conference recently, I had lunch with noted children's writer Rabbi Sandy Sasso (b. 1947), and I asked what her secret was for seeing the world through a child's eyes. She replied, "Let yourself be surprised."

Let your writing surprise you. Don't tell it what to do or order it around as if you were a staff sergeant. Instead, let yourself leap toward whatever gives you joy and try to remember how you saw things as a child, unfiltered and with wonder. Let one hand clap. Calm down … observe everything … let each moment creep up on you and, in its own way, startle you.

Exercises

- Close your eyes for one minute or longer. Breathe deeply. Then open your eyes and notice every object around you as if you'd never seen it before. (See my list of images I noticed from my office window, as an example.)
- Can you think of the last moment or experience that really surprised you? If not, be aware, throughout your day, of the small details that take you by surprise.
- *Poem assignment.* Think of your earliest childhood memory of experiencing joy. In a poem, describe the scene or in some way recapture that feeling.

Reading

Helpful Resources

- One of the most moving presentations of aesthetic joy and its connection to God is found in C. S. Lewis's memoir *Surprised by Joy: The Shape of My Early Life* (1955).

Classic Poets

- The Zen-influenced poets of Japan have a knack for constantly surprising the reader. You owe it to yourself to read the haiku of Kobayashi Issa. One of the best volumes is *Cup-of-Tea Poems* (1991), translated by haiku authority David Lanoue.
- Childlikeness and constant surprise—along with razor-sharp satire—epitomize the work of English poet Stevie

Smith (1902–1971). She also doodled illustrations to some of her poems. Find *All the Poems* (2016) for her complete works or *Best Poems* (1983) for an outstanding selection, both from New Directions.

Contemporary Poets

- For sheer surprise, I love the poems in the young-adult volume *God Went to Beauty School* (2003) by Newbery award–winning children's writer Cynthia Rylant (b. 1954). Though controversial in some circles, the book never fails to astonish, amuse, and touch the heart all at the same time.
- American poet Charles Ghigna (b. 1946) has excelled in writing poems that take a child's-eye-view of the world. Find his *Animal Tracks: Wild Poems to Read Aloud* (2004) or *Tickle Day: Poems from Father Goose* (1994).

All my poems are really love poems.
Rosemarie Waldrop[1]
(b. 1935)

10

Love and Loss: Red Hearts, Green Lights

Having looked at the senses, emotions, the imagination, dreams, childhood, and sudden insights as nourishers of poems, we now turn to love. Which may be one of the most potent but problematic sources of all.

Have you ever tried to write a good love poem? It's difficult. For one thing, it's a ruse because you're ostensibly writing to the loved one, but you're letting the whole world look over your shoulder. It's a cagey sort of stunt, like kissing your date on the kiss cam at the basketball game.

The Pre-Raphaelite painter and poet Dante Gabriel Rossetti (1828–1882) was determined to avoid that caginess when it came to the poems he'd written for his wife, Elizabeth Siddal (1829–1862), a poet, a painter in her own right, and the model for many of Rossetti's paintings. When Siddal died of an overdose of laudanum at age thirty-two, Rossetti deposited in her coffin a notebook containing the poems he'd written for her, many of which were unique copies. It was a supreme, romantic gesture after what had been a complicated relationship, to say the least.

Seven years later, needing to expand a collection of his poetry for his publisher, he remembered those poems—and wished he hadn't buried them. So, the coffin was dug up and the notebook retrieved. Siddal, according to the gravediggers, was as beautiful in death as in life—only that her luxurious red hair, as they reported, had continued to grow and now filled the coffin. (Shudder.)

Traffic Patterns

When I was in my mid-twenties, just when I thought I'd outgrown supreme romantic gestures, a woman named Paige proved me wrong. We met in graduate school. At the time, she was working on a degree in highway administration, and the subject of her thesis was the timing of traffic lights. I joked with friends that I was seeing a woman who spent a lot of time on street corners.

After we'd dated for a while, I had an inspiration. I would write a poem for her every day for a month, after which I would collect them into a little book. And so I did. A poem a day—thirty of them—which I hand-bound into a gift-size hardcover volume. Of course, unlike Rossetti, I kept a duplicate copy for myself. No telling when I might later need to expand an edition of my poems.

As you no doubt foresaw, on presentation day, Paige blinked me the big red light: "You know, you're very sweet, but, you see, I've just run into an old boyfriend ...," and suddenly, the traffic pattern was clear.

What surprised me even more was my own relief. Writing a love poem every day is hard work and a *big* commitment—not unlike marriage. And by poem number thirty, I'd realized something: I didn't want to write another word for Paige any more than I wanted to wake up next to her every morning for the rest of my life.

As a coda to that story, years later, Shelley, the women I *do love* waking up next to every morning (and an award-winning poet, by the way), was cleaning out a drawer and found those old poems. Instead of being angry or jealous, her comment was "Wow, these are really bad!"

"Well," I replied, "you had to know Paige!"

Love Poetry

Maybe such poems are easier for you than they are for me, but I'd be happy to discover that all my old love poems were securely padlocked in a rusty locker in a junior high school somewhere, which, with any luck, will soon burn to the ground.

Love poems can seem so juvenile, so unseemly. Somewhere in his *ABC of Reading*, American poet Ezra Pound (1885–1972) warns poets against even using the word *love* as a form of address (as in Shakespeare's "Sonnet 40": "Take all my loves, my love, yea take them all")[2] until they are acknowledged masters of the poetic craft. Used by lesser poets, the word is almost a one-word cliché, reminding me of the old Daffy Duck cartoon in which his wife lists for him all the chores she expects him to do; without looking up from his newspaper, Daffy intones: "Yes, m'love. Yes, m'love. Yes, m'love."

In addition, expressing deep affection for another person leaves us vulnerable—especially in a time like ours defined by irony and cynicism. Ours in not an age of sincerity, which makes it hard to take love poems seriously. In fact, most of the poets I know avoid writing such poems the way vampires avoid tanning salons. Some of our greatest poets seldom attempted poems for a lover or a spouse: the Chinese hermit poets, John Milton, William Blake, Wilfred Owen, T. S. Eliot, Ezra Pound, Stevie Smith, John Betjeman, Sylvia Plath, just to name a few. The late Gregory Corso (1930–2001) summarized the quandary in his poem "Marriage":

> O but what about love? I forget love
> not that I am incapable of love
> It's just that I see love as odd as wearing shoes—

I never wanted to marry a girl who was like my mother
And Ingrid Bergman was always impossible[3]

Memento Mori

Who needs love poems when they're as odd as wearing shoes?

But loving anything leaves us vulnerable in another way—vulnerable to losing it. As I paged back through at a lot of old poetry anthologies, a pattern started to emerge. Many of the great love poems aren't really about love. As often as not, they are about the prospect of losing the object of one's love—or having already lost it. Death, whether in past or future tense, intensifies the emotion. The Romans called it *memento mori,* "the remembrance of mortality," what English poet Andrew Marvell (1621–1678) termed "Time's wingèd chariot drawing near" (from "To His Coy Mistress"). Consider some other examples:

- In that same poem, Marvell says, "The grave's a fine and private place, / But none, I think, do there embrace."[4]
- In "Bright Star," John Keats (1795–1821) longs to lay his head on his lover's breast and "hear her tender-taken breath, / And so live ever—or else swoon to death."[5]
- The lovers in "Counting the Beats" by Robert Graves (1895–1985) feel, in their embrace, "The bleeding to death of time in slow heart beats."[6]
- In "You Are the Ruler of This Realm of Flesh," Dylan Thomas says, "The heart steps to death's finger."[7]
- Thomas Hardy (1840–1928) wrote an entire collection, *Poems 1912–13*, for his late wife, Emma Gifford. In one poem, he believes he senses her presence standing behind him, but he thinks, "to keep down grief / I would not turn my head to discover / That there was nothing in my belief."[8]

And on and on. Love grows not only in the sunlight of life but in death's shadow as well. It's a theme that runs through Shakespeare and John Donne and Edgar Allan Poe and countless others. That theme is a staple of pop songs. One of my favorite examples is Bruce Springsteen's "Wreck on the Highway."[9] The narrator is driving home late one night when he comes upon an accident scene. He stops to help a dying man who has been thrown from his car. A short time later, as the ambulance pulses away into the distance with the victim's lifeless body inside, the song's narrator thinks about the man's wife or lover who will receive a phone call later that night. Then he heads for home, where a shift takes place. As he looks at his sleeping wife, he shivers—one of those long, deep, existential shivers. And he thinks of how much he loves her. Simple and blunt, as pop songs can be, but it makes its point.

This whole idea is epitomized by that strange little myth about Cupid and the Angel of Death—who, one day, had their own mythic wreck on the highway. After having an accidental mid-air collision, they inadvertently pick up each other's quiver of arrows. Thereafter, Cupid flits around unknowingly shooting young lovers full of death arrows, and the Angel of Death gloomily pokes the aged with darts of desire and longing. It gives you chills. It's *Romeo and Juliet* and Barbry Ellen in the old folk ballad. It's Evelyn Waugh's novel *The Loved One*, it's a lot of blues music, and it's Orpheus and Eurydice. Dante's beloved Beatrice may well have toured him through Paradise—but she had to die first to get there. Whole religions have been built on death as the soil from which love springs.

As witnesses to the marriage of love and loss, Japanese poets write about cherry blossoms—they are almost obsessed with the trope—not just because cherry blossoms are beautiful, but because they are also short-lived, a metaphor for everything we hold dear in this ephemeral life.

The Case for Love Poems

So here's the point. How deeply have you thought about whom you love—and what you love—and about the prospect of losing them? Love and grieving, in some toweringly universal and interconnected way, are emotions that have animated poetry since the beginning of recorded time. In fact, humankind's earliest extant work of literature, *The Epic of Gilgamesh*, is about just that. King Gilgamesh of Uruk loves his friend Enkidu so deeply that when Enkidu dies, Gilgamesh sets off on a half-crazed journey to unlock life's mysteries and seek the secret of immortality.

Consider German poet Friedrich Rückert (1788–1866) who wrote more than four hundred poems of lament after his two children died from disease. Later, in 1904, composer Gustav Mahler set five of those poems to music as the heartrending cycle *Songs on the Death of Children*. In the third of those songs, the poet speaks to the deceased daughter, saying that when her mother enters the room, he does not look at the mother's face, but rather he gazes at her side, where the young girl's face would have been.

Or consider an old Chinese poem, in which the poet gleefully gives his beloved grandmother a piggy-back ride just for a lark. Then, in an instant, he weeps to realize how light she is, how frail and close to death.

In our time, consider poet and children's writer Jane Yolen (b. 1939). When her husband was diagnosed with a brain tumor, he underwent forty-three days of radiation treatment. Yolen's response was to write a sonnet each day, for forty-three days, as a way to cope with her love and possible loss. Her beautiful, unsentimental, but often funny and hopeful poems were published as *The Radiation Sonnets* (2003), a favorite volume of cancer survivors everywhere.

Love poems, as I said, are difficult. Far easier is it to write intellectual poems that skitter on the surface of life, make sly observations, and display one's poetic bravura. There's a place for those kinds of poems, and I'm certainly not dismissing them. I've written my share. But on some level, *all* poems are love poems, even the object of that love is one's own cleverness.

But how satisfying is that really? Sooner or later, most poets find it necessary to sink into that deep prayerful silence we spoke of in chapter 3. Sooner or later, you may find it necessary to let your own deepest turmoil about love and loss, desire and grief, longing and lament speak *to* you—and then *through* you in your poems.

Ponder these lines from the most famous poem by Victorian poet Elizabeth Barrett Browning (1806–1861), the one that begins "How do I love thee? Let me count the ways," a poem often overlooked by scholars, perhaps for being too well-known. But her lines are not a formal exercise in sonnet-making, nor are they sentimental tripe. They are a true heart's cry:

> I love thee with the passion put to use
> In my old griefs, and with my childhood's faith.
> I love thee with a love I seemed to lose
> With my lost saints.[10]

Facing our loves and losses can be uncomfortable, a caustic kind of self-therapy, leading us into a soul-hollowing but salutary vulnerability. But perhaps now is the time to do that work—the work of poems—to discover who you are by opening yourself to those emotions and anxieties honestly, and, like Gilgamesh, to take that half-crazed epic journey of desperate love.

Exercises

- Take some time alone to think deeply about who and what you most love in your life at the moment—and what the prospect of losing them (of having already lost them) might mean.

- *Poem assignment:* Write a love poem for someone—but write it for that person alone, with no other reader over your shoulder as you write it and no intention of ever publishing it. In the poem, list those moments when you most feel that love, and share the anxiety you have about losing—or about having already lost—that love.

Reading

Helpful Resources

- Roger Housden has compiled an outstanding collection of poems about love in its most spiritual aspects: *Risking Everything: 110 Poems of Love and Revelation* (Harmony, 2003). Also good is Housden's anthology with short introductions, *Twenty Poems to Bless Your Marriage* (2012).
- Kevin Young's outstanding anthology, *The Art of Losing: Poems of Grief and Healing* (2013) is an excellent resource for studying how poets handle the emotions surrounding death and loss.
- Drawing on classic and contemporary poets, Scottish poet Carol Ann Duffy (b. 1952) has compiled a lovely anthology called *Stopping for Death: Poems of Death and Loss* (1996), containing many poems on the subject of love and grief—a surprising mix of tragedy, insight, and humor.

Classic Poets

- Pablo Neruda's *Love Poems* (New Directions, 1973), bilingual edition, English translations by Donald D. Walsh. As an added bonus, track down the 1994 Italian film *Il Postino* (*The Postman)*, which is based on the story of Neruda mentoring a young postman in the art of writing love poems for his beloved. It's charming and beautiful (available on disc from Amazon).

Contemporary Poet

- American poet of Chinese descent Li-Young Lee (b. 1957) has written beautifully about his wife and his later father's blindness and death in his collection *Rose* (1993).

I love your hills, and I love your
dales,
And I love your flocks a-bleating—
But O, on the heather to lie
together
With both our hearts a-beating.
—John Keats
(1795–1821)[1]

11

Love and Sex: A Brief, Comic Interlude

The Poetry Section used to be the most secluded spot in our busy local bookstore. Whenever I needed to escape the cloying smell of over-sweetened cappuccino, the loitering masses at the magazine racks, the painfully furtive in the Psychology/Self-help Section, or the earnestly dreamy in Metaphysics—I could always head to the Poetry shelves for privacy. No one was ever there.

Few people read, let alone buy, poetry, it seems—which has its benefits when you're feeling reclusive. Poets tend to be recluses, like Ovid on the Black Sea, Sappho on Lesbos, or Yeats dreaming of Innisfree. The secluded isles/aisles call us, and we respond.

Love and Sex

But all that changed a few years ago when that same bookseller moved their entire stock to a new and larger location.[2] The Poetry Section was now situated in a neat little alcove, well-lit with a classy wooden bench, floor-to-ceiling bookcases, and a wheeled ladder to reach the highest shelves. What could be better?

Well, solitude for one thing.

Soon I noticed that whenever I went to the Poetry Section for some reflective browsing, someone was sitting on that bench—a different person each time, mind you, but it happened with unnerving regularity.

With a bit of over-the-shoulder snooping I figured out the reason for these invasions: the Poetry alcove was now around the corner from the one marked Love & Sex.

What was happening was this: if you're an attractive young co-ed who wants to browse through *227 Ways to Unleash the Sex Goddess Within* (yes, it's an actual book), the last thing you want is to tempt some guy to try out the pickup line "Read any good books lately?" So you take your reading elsewhere. Next door to Poetry.

Or if you're a lonely graduate student who wants to sneak a peek at the *Complete Idiot's Guide to the Kama Sutra* (also a real book), where are you going to sit? Certainly *not* in the big easy chair in Love & Sex where everyone will see you. No, you head to Poetry.

I made a game of this at times, deliberately disrupting the scene. Just having someone browse among the poetry books was usually enough to make the most hardcore fantasist flee. If that didn't work, I'd pull a volume off the shelves—a *large* one, like Whitman's *Leaves of Grass*—and sit down near the person and start at page one. That did the trick. At other times the interloper just seemed too fragile, too lonely to interrupt. So, taking pity, I'd head over to Audio Books to see what was shaking in the way of poetry there.

Apparently, I'm not the only one who makes these readers nervous. I often find evidence that the expatriates from Love & Sex have had to make quick getaways. I'd often find material bordering on the pornographic lurking among the books on the poetry shelves—volumes that were abandoned there, no doubt, when things got too steamy and the reader had to catch some fresh air elsewhere. How often I've found something like

The Good Girl's Guide to Bad Girl Sex (real) nestled next to the volumes of Milton. And what would *he* have thought?

Sex in Poetry

I sympathize with these refugees from Love & Sex because I've been there too. I was a lonely graduate student myself once, studying poetry and world literature. And I now wish I had the courage to tell these folks that they could learn everything they want to know about sex and love and relationships and more sex and passion and even more sex from poems!

I could have pulled from the shelf the wonderful anthology *The Erotic Spirit: An Anthology of Poems of Sensuality, Love, and Longing* (1999), edited by poet Sam Hamill (b. 1943), and I could have said, "Here. Read this. It's good." Or how about *Passionate Hearts: The Poetry of Sexual Pleasure: An Anthology* (1996), edited by sex therapist Wendy Maltz (b. 1950)? For the religiously inclined, there's the marvelous translation of *The Song of Songs* (1993) by poet and painter Marcia Falk (b. 1946). It's one of my favorites. And need I mention "Song of Myself" by Walt Whitman (1819–1892)? In one place he describes listening to an operatic soprano this way: "She convulses me like the climax of my love-grip"? (Whitman, though a favorite of Abraham Lincoln's, was considered a brown-paper-cover kind of writer by many in the nineteenth century.)

It's all there, and it has been the stuff of poetry ever since Sappho (c. 630–c. 570 BCE), Catullus (c. 84–c. 54 BCE), Propertius (c. 50–15 BCE), Ovid (43 BCE–18 CE), John Wilmot, Earl of Rochester (1647–1680), and so many others. Do these readers know that Charles Bukowski (1920–1994), perhaps the most pornographic poet to walk the earth, and Anne Sexton (1928–1974) and the Japanese poetess Yosano Akiko (1878–1942) and American poet Ruth Stone (1915–2011) and so many other great *sexy* poets are right there? Right under their noses?

Lit. Crit.

All this got me thinking about the other bookstores I frequent and what subjects they plop next to *their* Poetry Sections, for I suspected that these juxtapositions are external expressions of some ingrained attitudes about poetry.

For instance, ... at our old Barnes & Noble, before they moved, Literary Criticism was adjacent to Poetry. (And both were next to the restrooms! How's that for interesting?) The proximity of Lit. Crit. made me realize that for many people, poetry is a largely academic pursuit—meant for the poetry professionals that we've been talking about. Some of my dearest friends are brilliant poetry scholars. They have studied poetry far more systematically than I could ever hope to, and I'm surprised at how often they even explain my own poetry to me! But for them, poetry is Lit. Crit. more often than not.

In contrast to these wonderful, insightful scholars are the other kind. Several years ago, while I was in the midst of writing an essay about American poet Edna St. Vincent Millay (1892–1950), I discovered that renowned critic Richard Ellman omitted her from his hefty *Oxford Book of American Verse.* It seemed baffling until I realized that in Ellman's mental bookstore too, Poetry is adjacent to Lit. Crit.—and the critics of the past fifty years have not been kind to Dame Millay. She's too messy, too melodramatic, too throbbing with hormones and bile and sex. And ultimately, she was too popular. In her lifetime, she outsold her contemporaries Ezra Pound and T. S. Eliot put together—several times over. And popularity is often something that scholars have a hard time forgiving. Think of other wonderful (though less sexy) poets who are also usually overlooked by the Lit. Crit. academy: Robert Louis Stevenson, Rudyard Kipling, Ogden Nash, Dorothy Parker, Don Marquis, and Phyllis McGinley. All brilliant at their best but too popular to impress the critics.

Classics, Fiction, Sci-Fi, and More

In another local bookstore, which has since gone out of business, Poetry was folded into Classics, which is common in smaller stores, I've found. You've known folks who have that mindset. Poetry is *classic*, something you studied in school. They read a lot of poetry but no living poets. I knew a dear woman who claimed to *hate* modern poetry, even though I doubt that she'd read more than two poems by living poets. She was, I might add, a former English teacher. A teacher of the classics.

In some bookstores, like our newly reconfigured Barnes & Noble, Poetry is now squeezed in at the end of Fiction. Like a footnote, an afterthought. Some readers of popular fiction view poetry this way—as the "other" genre of literature that one ought to get around to reading one of these days. After all, some novelists have written poetry too. Right? Victor Hugo, Herman Melville, Thomas Hardy, Robert Graves, Jack Kerouac, John Updike, Louise Erdrich. *Maybe I should check it out sometime*, these readers think. But when they do, they are often disappointed. Why is it so hard to make out the story? Why is the language so indirect? Because, well, it's not fiction. And your years of speed-reading are not an asset.

Another store I know of used to have their Poetry back-to-back with the Science Fiction/Fantasy shelves, which is an intriguing thought. It makes me think of *Idylls of the King*, the Arthurian epic by Alfred, Lord Tennyson (1809–1892) or *The Wanderings of Oisin*, a Celtic myth, by W. B. Yeats (1865–1939). J. R. R. Tolkien (1892–1973) wrote a fair amount of poetry himself and even translated a number of medieval poems like *Sir Gawain and the Green Knight* and *Beowulf*.

It's also pleasant to think of the bookstore in the town where I grew up, where Poetry was next to Travel. My late parents loved the exotic travel verse of Don Blanding (1894–1957), who was the Jimmy Buffett of poetry back in the 1940s and '50s, writing verse about setting sail toward the tropic isles. Poetry as escape.

Our Inner Selves and Our Inner Shelves

As poets, we tend to put some interesting "sections" next to Poetry in our mental bookstores (I've been guilty of all of the following). We write poetry to get a handle on our stresses and undefined emotions (Psychology/Self-Help), to project an image of ourselves to others (Biography), to figure out the nature of reality (Philosophy), to get a laugh (Humor), as a form of prayer or worship (Religion & Spirituality), as a form of protest (Politics), or to just keep our minds active and engaged as we age (Fitness).

In the old days, when there used to be a lot more small independent bookstores with names like "The Book Stop" and "Booktique," Poetry was invariably placed on the bottom shelf beneath Gift-and-Inspirational. I admit that these stores were, on many occasions, akin to my own mental makeup. I make the writing of poetry into an almost monastic discipline—a certain number of lines each day, a delving into the spiritual, a striving for a kind of language that is always bordering on prayer, a way of "thinking" my way into heaven. What's more, I like to make gifts of my poetry! In my mental bookstore, my worst, most sentimental poetry is on that sanctimonious little bottom shelf. (You'll recall my hand-bound volume for Paige.)

For the person who writes poetry, the problem with "Gift and Inspirational"—as well as "Lit. Crit.," "Fiction," "Classics," "Philosophy," and whatever else—is that they tend toward the cerebral, the clever, displays of mental agility. They are valid, of course, and needful—all of them—but they are incomplete in themselves. And, sad to say, too often sterile. Kierkegaard's shortest written prayer was "Lord, keep me from intellectual prayers"—and that from one of the greatest intellectuals of the last two hundred years. The corollary is obvious: "Lord, keep me from intellectual poems."

Bringing It All Back Home

Which brings us back to Love & Sex. Let's face it, that topic has the greatest potential for driving the poet (and anyone else, for that matter) mad. It can lead people astray into the realms of unhealthy fantasy, sex-addiction, internet porn, sexual harassment, and criminality. The great majority of our relational mess-ups in life—if literature and the newspapers are to be believed—stem from those two subjects.

But that's the point: the incredible potency of those subjects is what also grants them the greatest potential for leading us back to reality. To everyday relationships. To marriage. To affection and crushes. To commitment. To ecstasy and joy. To overcoming fear and vulnerability and isolation. Love & Sex is how we got here in the first place, and it's at the heart of the mystery of life. Love & Sex reminds us that the emotions are not only central to poetry, but to life. That's why the Songs of Songs is in the Bible and why it's listed as one of the *Poetic* Books.

Love & Sex, whether we like it or not, is our home address. It can help us see more clearly, to not think too little or too much or ourselves. It makes us human by covering all the emotional terrain between the profound tragedy of Shakespeare's *Romeo and Juliet* to the giddy teasing of Mozart's Pappagheeno and Pappagheena in *The Magic Flute*.

I once taught a college class in poetry. One of the poems in the anthology we were using was a poem by the Sung Dynasty poet Tseng Kung (1019–1083). In it, the aging scholar-poet climbs a high tower at the Kan-lu monastery to take in the views. At the top, he can just scent the breeze of the far-off ocean, and he longs to set sail. As he gazes into the distance, he concludes the poem with two of my favorite lines in all of Chinese poetry:

> Though I am old, the dust of the world clings to my robe;
> I wish only to admire the high-flying geese.[3]

Full of confidence about Confucianism and contemplation, I asked the class what they thought the poem was about. One women, a beautiful, gray-haired woman more than twice my age, said, "Sex." I did a double take, but she proceeded to deliver a spontaneous lecture that was far better than anything I'd prepared. She interpreted the tower in the expected Freudian way, but more intriguingly, she said the poem was about the aged poet remembering the sexual feelings of his youth but no longer being able to experience them. That is what the dust of the world and the high-flying geese are all about. As I read back through the rest of the poem, it all fell into place. My mind had been in Lit. Crit. and partially in Travel, while hers was where the poet intended. In Love & Sex.

Where Do We Go from Here?

So, have you read many poets who talk about sex? These are poets who are not ashamed to have their Poetry Sections right next to Love & Sex. These are poets who—whether they succeeded at life and love or not—made it their business to attend to the real world. They are also poets who, I suspect, do not go to the Poetry Section to be alone. They would not have a snobbish attitude about the lonely college kid reading dirty books there. These poets wouldn't just think about offering an appropriate book of poetry, they would offer an original poem.

So, every year, on Valentine's Day at the very least, we should remind ourselves to move our poetry back to its original location, to box up the books from "Gift and Inspirational" and let them breathe the risky but wildly refreshing air in Love & Sex.

It's time to make the move.

Exercises

- Think deeply about your own mental attitude toward poetry. What section of the bookstore is next to your poetry section?
- Look over your best poems from the past. How has your approach changed? More or less vulnerability? More or less intellectualism? More or less genuine emotion?
- *Poem Assignment:* What is your earliest memory of sexual attraction, either as a child or an adolescent? Write a poem that captures that time and that feeling as honestly as possible.

Reading

Helpful Resources

- A good collection of poems from the Love & Sex section is *The Erotic Spirit: An Anthology of Poems of Love, Sensuality, and Longing*, compiled by poet Sam Hamill (b. 1947).

Classic Poets

- Roman classical literature is full of very sensual love poetry by such poets as Catullus (c. 84–c. 54 BCE) or Sextus Propertius (c. 50–c. 15 BCE). One of the best known is the *Amores* ("the Loves") by Ovid (43 BCE–18 CE). His subsequent, even more scandalous volume, the *Ars Amatoria* ("The Art of Love"), may have contributed to his being exiled to the Black Sea by Caesar Augustus.

- Japanese poet Yosano Akiko (1878–1942) was noted for the passion of her poems. Find translations of her poems by Sam Hamill in *River of Stars: Selected Poems of Yosano Akiko* (1997).

Contemporary Poets

- Pablo Neruda was never far from the Love & Sex section. Master American poet W. S. Merwin (b. 1927) has done a splendid translation of Neruda's *Twenty Love Poems and a Song of Despair* (1993).
- As mentioned in the chapter, find *Passionate Hearts: The Poetry of Sexual Love: An Anthology* (1996) compiled by Wendy Maltz.

> Rhymes, meters, stanza forms, etc., are like servants. If the master is fair enough to win their affection and firm enough to command their respect, the result is an orderly happy household.
>
> —W. H. Auden (1907–1973)[1]

12

Rhyme, Meter, and Forms: Racquetball in the Caves of Lascaux

Unlike the other chapters in this book, this one begins with its conclusions:

- If you believe a poem must rhyme to be a poem, then you may need to stop right now and write a couple of free-verse poems.
- If you write only free verse, then you should try your hand at a sonnet or a villanelle.
- Whatever kind of poetry you write, you owe it to yourself to have a basic grasp of the technical aspects of form, meter, and rhyme—all part of what's called prosody. Even abstract painters study the fundamentals of representational drawing. You have to know the rules to break the rules.

If those suggestions make sense—and if you're already well-versed in the basics of prosody—then skip the rest of this chapter. If not, read on.

The Case for Formal Poetry

Dedicated readers of poetry are seldom picky about whether they read formal verse or free verse. For them, poems are poems, and Walt Whitman (America's archetypal free-verse poet) is as legitimate as Emily Dickinson (a formal-verse writer), just as Langston Hughes (a free verser) is as legitimate as Mona Van Duyn (who wrote mostly rhymed verse).

But the poets themselves are often more obdurate. For instance, many books about poetry sooner or later get around to quoting G. K. Chesterton (1874–1936) who once quipped, "'Free verse'? You may as well call sleeping in a ditch 'free architecture'"; and those same books invariably quote Robert Frost (1874–1963), who famously said that writing a poem that doesn't rhyme is like "playing tennis without a net."[2]

For the past forty years, American literature has witnessed a resurgence of formal poetry due to the rise of an energetic Neo-Formalist movement, which includes poets like Lewis Turco (b. 1934), Dana Gioia (b. 1950), Molly Peacock (b. 1947), Mark Jarman (b. 1952), and others. In 1992, Gioia published an influential collection of essays, *Can Poetry Matter? Essays on Poetry and American Culture*, which has become a seminal document for the movement and for modern poetry in general.

These poets cite many reasons for their preference, among which are these:

1. **Limits.** Many poets prefer formal verse, paradoxically, because they find greater freedom within its parameters. Structure suggests possibilities. Like playing tennis with a net, meter and rhyme set boundaries and make the rules clear, and unlimited freedom can be another term for chaos. W. H. Auden (1907–1973) compared

free-verse writers to Robinson Crusoe who, on his tropical island, had to do everything for himself and create everything from scratch. Sometimes "this manly independence," writes Auden of free-verse poets, "produces something original and impressive, but more often the result is squalor—dirty sheets on the unmade bed and empty bottles on the unswept floor."[3]

The structural limitations of formal verse also require the poet to lean heavily on the intellect. The poet does not so much write a sonnet as construct one. The process requires a certain puzzle-solving skill in calculating how to sequence the rhymes, when to vary the meter, where to insert the pauses, and so on. This process of focusing the mind on architectural technique, so the theory goes, allows deeper emotions to emerge on their own. Shakespeare's sonnets are a supreme example.

2. **Music.** Formal poetry is spoken music. The rhymes and meters, of course, contribute to their musicality, but such poems also often have an elegant lilt all their own. Listen to a recording of Dylan Thomas, for example, reading the poems of W. B. Yeats (1865–1939)[4]—but turn the volume down so that you can hear only the humming of the lines without distinguishing the words, and you'll know you're listening to great music. Or pick up a copy of Milton's *Paradise Lost*, open it randomly, and start reciting aloud. Milton's blank verse is so rich as to be almost symphonic. T. S. Eliot (1888–1965) wrote that "genuine poetry can communicate before it's understood."[5] He recalled reading the opening lines of Dante's *Inferno* for the first time—even before he knew Italian—and being overwhelmed by the sheer beauty of sound, its cadence and elegance:

Nel mezzo del cammin di nostra vita
me ritrovai per una selva oscura
ché la diritta via era smaritta.[6]

3. **Tradition.** For nearly seven centuries, European poetry was dominated by traditional forms—songs, odes, ballads, sonnets, blank verse, and more—all of which have regular meter and (except for blank verse) rhyme. Forms link contemporary poetry to a great tradition, giving it authority.

4. **Memorization.** Rhyme and meter help us remember poems. Think of your favorites. Of those you've memorized, I suspect at least nine out of ten contain rhyme and regular meter. Despite our having lived in the age of free verse for more than a century, the vast majority of poems in Robert Pinsky's Favorite Poem Project (chosen by readers online) are rhyming ones. The simple reason is that they're easier to remember. The late poet Daniel Abdal-Hayy Moore (1940–2016) once wrote to me, "How many people can recite 'The Charge of the Light Brigade,' and how many can recite a William Carlos Williams or a Charles Olson poem by heart?"

You may recall marine biologist Roger Payne, who, back in the sixties, first studied and recorded actual whale songs. Singer Judy Collins, on one of her albums, recorded the whaling song "Farewell to Tarwathie" to the accompaniment of those whale songs, and Payne's recordings were included on that golden disc aboard the Voyager space probes. Here's the point: Payne and his colleagues discovered that whales repeat similar sounds at regular intervals, and the longer the whale song, the more the same sound is repeated. Payne's hypothesis? Whales use rhyme as a way to remember their songs.

5. **Magic.** As mentioned in chapter 7 ("Magic and Imagination"), meter and rhyme have roots in ancient incantation. Whether it's the black magic of "Abracadabra" and "hocus-pocus" or the white magic of "I wish I may, I wish I might," words have power. Latin was the preferred language of wizards not only because both the Catholic Church and medieval alchemical texts used it, but also because, having a somewhat limited number of end-sounds, Latin is a language rich in rhymes, granting it both musicality and mystery.

6. **Inevitability.** Professor and E. E. Cummings scholar Michael Webster of Grand Valley State University suggests that meter and rhyme lend inevitability to a poem. They make the words sound as if they are saying exactly what they were meant to say, as though they couldn't have been constructed any other way. Hardly a parent hasn't played that game with their child: reading lines of poetry and leaving out the last word for the child to fill in. The words are inescapable.

7. **Humor.** While the inevitability of rhyme can be elegant, it can also be comic, which everyone from Chaucer to Chesterton, from Byron to Billy Collins, understood. Children who grew up on *Where the Sidewalk Ends* by Shel Silverstein (1930–1999) know the joy of clever and unexpected rhymes. There's also a delight in a crisp epigram in which the final, precise rhyme sends the rapier jab home. Consider Samuel Taylor Coleridge's own epigram about epigrams: "What is an Epigram?

a dwarfish whole, / its body brevity, and wit its soul." Such verse can be dangerous, however; Coleridge's own grandmother wrote him out of her will after he wrote a comic epigram about her beard![7]

The Case against Rhyme and Meter

A case can also be made against formal verse. Anyone who has listened to a well-meaning uncle propose a versified toast at a family wedding knows how appalling rhyme and meter can be when badly done. Some people—especially those who don't read much poetry—assume that by just making words rhyme, they are writing a poem. They jumble the syntax to push the rhyming words to the end of each line, and they create a heavy-handed rhythm in what is unkindly referred to as "tub-thumping": *boom da-da-boom da-da-boom da BOOM*. Even the ancient Greek philosopher Aristotle noted his distaste for such amateur versifying by refusing to consider the physician Empedocles a poet, despire the fact that his scientific treatises were written in Homeric hexameter.[8]

A pastor I once knew delivered a verse sermon on the life of Saint Peter, though it was not just ordinary verse. He chose to rhyme the entire sermon using just one rhyme, with every line ending in " –ight," so that it sounded something like this (I'm reconstructing a portion from memory):

> Through that dismal night
> Peter stood by the fire's light
> shaking with emotion and fright
> having denied the Savior outright
> not once but thrice and then in spite
> of the Savior having foreseen it aright …

And so on, as though Bottom the weaver had turned gospel writer. Not only did we hear a couple of hundred of rhymes in

"–ight" in the course of fifteen minutes, but when he was done, the minister explained with a twinkle in his eye, "Those of you familiar with poetry [he glanced in my direction] will have noticed that I used just one rhyme throughout. That's a very difficult technical feat." It was endearingly awful.

Pre-Raphaelite writer and designer William Morris (1834–1896) had a different view of the difficulty of such verse. When he was twenty years old, he wrote his first poem, a thoroughly amateur, tub-thumping effort. When his friends complimented him effusively, he replied with surprising candor, "Well, if this is poetry, it is very easy to write."[9]

But of course, the cure for bad rhyming poetry is not free verse, which can be every bit as bad. Other, more salient reasons exist for avoiding formal verse.

Many free-verse poets argue that the rhyme and regular meter of fixed forms work against a poem's spontaneity, sincerity, and vitality. What the Neo-Formalist considers elegant, the free-verse poet calls artificial, too premeditated and too formulaic to elicit honest heartfelt expression.

Many free-verse poets also see formal verse in socio-political terms. They remind us that the familiar poetic forms like the sonnet, the ballad stanza, the villanelle, and so on, were developed in Europe, by societies that, at the same time, were colonial, culturally paternalistic, overbearing, and racist. Where the formalist sees tradition, the free-verse poet sees exploitation.

Furthermore, Frost's jab about "playing tennis without a net" is precisely why many modern poets reject rhyme. The kind of tennis that Frost had in mind was probably not the aggressive, hard-hitting game of Serena Williams or Roger Federer, but the clubby lawn-tennis of sunny Sunday afternoons in New England, a pastime, a social distraction for the elite. His tennis metaphor unwittingly perpetuates the idea of formal poetry as something genteel and refined, like string quartets or afternoon tea.[10] There's a whiff of classism about it.

But "playing tennis without a net" is a good description of another game: racquetball—and it is not at all inappropriate to compare free verse to that fast-paced, off-the-wall, free-for-all of a game. A lot of people, more agile and rigorous than Frost, prefer racquetball to tennis, so that you might say Walt Whitman was, metaphorically, one of the great racquetball players of all time.

A Middle Way

But racquetball, like free verse, isn't entirely free. There are still four walls, a ceiling, and a floor to hem in the game, just as there are limits to every free-verse poem. Whether those limits are the traditional "beginning, middle, and end" or just the trim size of the page the poem is printed on, a free verse poem exists within them. And Limitation Number One for any poem is, as always, that it communicates something to someone.

Although many poets only write one kind of poem, others cross the boundaries. Early in his career, Walt Whitman wrote rhymed verse. In fact, a lot poets write both kinds. Even T. S. Eliot, the great free-verse writer of the twentieth century, wrote his children's poems, *Old Possum's Book of Practical Cats*, in elegant and intricate rhymes.

Ultimately, the distinction between formal verse and free verse is artificial because both kinds of poetry require the poet to be acutely aware of the sounds and rhythms in what they are writing. Whether a poem strives for elegance in its music or for a kind of rugged anti-music, it is still music. *Howl* by Allen Ginsberg (1926–1997) is every bit as lyrical in its own rough way as *Paradise Lost* by John Milton (1608–1674). The charm, the magic, of poetry is still its aural quality, the way it sounds when spoken.

For me, it's about voice (which we will examine in more detail in the next chapter). For decades, I wrote largely, though not exclusively, fixed forms: sonnets, rondels, and long blank-verse narratives in particular. My voice in those poems imitated the formal poets I love, like W. B. Yeats, John Betjeman, Richard

Wilbur, Robert Graves, Edward Thomas, and many others. That voice was complex, traditional, a bit stuffy, and sophisticated—what might be called "Episcopalian." But when it came to writing the poems that grew into my first book, the voice was different; it was restless, ecstatic, pushy and abrupt, and deliberately unmusical—what might be called "street corner." I deliberately played against "pretty." Those poems were free verse, and in them I tried to echo the Beat poets of the 1950s, the hermit poets of China, the Sufi poets of the Middle East, and the anti-poets of Latin America. It was a different voice than I'd written in before. And I loved it.

In all cases, the content should determine the form. Whether your poetry is formal or free makes no difference as long as the form reinforces whatever you are trying to communicate. For example, you might have an idea for a poem that has two distinct parts, a sort of point/counterpoint, thesis/antithesis. That may be an indication that the Muse is telling you to write a sonnet, in which the first eight lines (the octave) state an idea, and the last six lines (the sestet) veer in a different direction. You may have two lines that are so good that they just keep repeating themselves in your mind, which may be the Muse suggesting a villanelle. If you have a particularly elegant idea, pentameter quatrains might be called for. A pithy quip calls for an epigram.

But you need to know the options so that you can recognize what form the Muse is whispering to you, whether that form is fixed or free. You may even invent your own form—and your own music—because that is what the voice and content of the poem demand.

Nature's Way

As a final note, I'd like to suggest that the source of poetic music is more ancient and more primal than the European colonialists. Poetry is part of the natural world.

I once heard a radio interview with a scientist named Stephen J. Waller, who described himself as an "acoustic archaeologist," or more precisely, a "biochemist and rock-art acoustician"—he studies the ways that ancient humans *heard* the world around them.[11]

His thesis is fascinating. For decades, archaeologists have puzzled over the mystery of why ancient humans chose certain locations and not others to depict their rock-art. Why, for instance, did hunters go so deeply into the caves of Lascaux, in southwestern France, seventeen thousand years ago to paint their herds of elk, bison, and horses on the walls? Why not some other, more accessible spot? Waller spent years studying more than a hundred such sites around the world to answer that question.

His conclusion: because of the echoes. Early artists chose certain sites because they believed echoes were the voices—the rumblings—of the spirits. At Lascaux, the paintings are located in the perfect spot where a particular effect is created when people clap their hands or stomp their feet. The echoes—in that spot—sound like stampeding hooves.

Likewise, Petroglyph National Park, near Albuquerque, is a location rich with unusual rock paintings, called petroglyphs. The best echoes in the park are found if you stand directly in front of any of those paintings. Remember the first time you heard a recording of your own voice and how *unlike* you it sounded? Now, imagine humans who had never heard recordings of their own voices and believed everything could be explained by the presence of spirits. To hear their own words rebounding back at them seemed supernatural. It was spirit magic. So they painted their art in those places to invoke those spirits.

Echo and rhyme are bound up together—especially in those humans' minds. Far from being an elite game for snobby poets, I wonder whether there isn't something organic and elemental about rhyme. It is the earth's way of speaking our own words back to us.

All around us, sounds repeat—and not just echoes. Owls hoot the same vowel sound in their call: "Who, who, who cooks for you." And then other owls answer them back. The black-capped chickadee says a rhymed poem with its call of "fee bee, fee bee."

Rhythms are found everywhere in nature: the sound of water flowing over stones in a stream; the patter of bird trills; the galloping of hooves; the hammering of the woodpecker; waves crashing into the shore, and so much more. John Keats, referring to a cricket's chirp, wrote, "the poetry of earth is never dead."[12]

Not all sounds in nature repeat, nor does everything echo or have a regular cadence. There is the sound of leaves in wind. There are growls and howls and thunder which seem random and unpredictable. Those I think of as nature's free verse.

All these sounds nourish our poetry because they are grounded in the world around us, as natural as the created order itself. Our poetic tradition does not go back to England or Rome or ancient China. It goes back to the thousands of places like the caves of Lascaux or just a bubbling stream where early humans heard something supernatural in the sounds around them.

We, as inheritors of nature's music, can write with rhyme and meter if we like—or not. But in either case, we can write with the assurance that we're not just playing a polite game of lawn tennis on a Sunday afternoon. We're playing racquetball in the caves of Lascaux.

Exercises

- Do you know the difference between a trochee and a spondee? Alliteration and consonance? Half rhyme and a para rhyme? If not, you need to read a quick-study guide like Octavia Wynne's *Poetic Meter and Form* (Wooden Books, 2016). (See "Readings" for other references.) Those terms aren't just bits of arcane information; they're helpful tools.[13]

- Grab a poetry anthology and read at least a half dozen poems that rhyme. Note that those poems are *not* about the rhyme. Those poets seldom strain their syntax to make the rhymes fit. In fact, you'll find that they often "write over" the rhymes at the ends of lines in a technique called "enjambment." They purposely deemphasize the rhymes. Note what the poems *are* about: elegance, balance, euphony, and depth of emotion.
- As an exercise, read several of those metered and rhyming poems aloud—but read them in as natural a speaking cadence as possible. Don't pause over the rhymes or emphasize the meter. Read them naturally as if they were prose or spoken monologues. Note how different poets handle those formal techniques.
- *Poem assignment:* Write a sonnet. Use traditional iambic pentameter. Feel the shape of the poem: the this/but, point/counterpoint structure. It is a challenge—and a discipline—to write a sonnet, but it is a valuable exercise.

Reading

Helpful Resources

- Octavia Wynne's charming hardcover *Poetic Meter and Form* (Wooden Books, 2016) is the most accessible introduction, and at 64 pages, it's one of the least expensive books on prosody. Also good and inexpensive is John Hollander's *Rhyme's Reason: A Guide to English Verse* (1989).
- Robin Skelton's *Shapes of Our Singing: A Comprehensive Guide to Verse Forms and Meters from Around the World* (Eastern Washington Univ., 2002) is an excellent

midsize guide. Robert Hass's *A Little Book on Form* (HarperCollins, 2017) and Edward Hirsch's *A Poet's Glossary* (Houghton Mifflin, 2014) are excellent comprehensive guides. Also helpful is Mark Strand and Eavan Boland's *The Making of a Poem: A Norton Anthology of Poetic Forms* (Norton, 2001).

- No poet should be without a good rhyming dictionary. The best one on the market is *Words to Rhyme With* (2001) by the late master wordsmith Willard R. Espy.

Classic Poets

- Reading Shakespeare's sonnets is a must, not just for their formal aspects but also for the depth of their emotional power. If you haven't read them since high school, don't put it off. They're available in dozens of editions, but I recommend the well-annotated *Shakespeare's Sonnets* (2010) in the Arden Shakespeare series, or for a thoroughly annotated edition with insightful commentary, find Helen Vendler's *The Art of Shakespeare's Sonnets* (1997).
- Most poetry written before the First World War was formal poetry. Among the many more recent poets who wrote at least some formal verse as often as not, my favorites are Theodore Roethke (1908–1963), Richard Wilbur (1921–2017), Phillip Larkin (1922–1985), and Seamus Heaney (1939–2013).

Contemporary Poets

- *To the Green Man* (2004) by Mark Jarman (b. 1952) is a good example of contemporary Neo-Formalism.
- Also find *Interrogations at Noon* (2001) by Dana Gioia (b. 1950).

Don't use the phone. People are never ready to answer it. Use poetry.

—Jack Kerouac[1]

13 Voices and a Voice: The Mocking Bird's Song

On a steamy summer night in North Carolina, I couldn't sleep. A mocking bird was perched in the tree outside my apartment window, and although I could have shooed it away, I didn't. I was mesmerized. It sang no song twice but strung together one brilliant burst after another—a medley that was, as music critics say, "a bravura performance."

I have since learned that mocking birds can imitate anywhere from forty to two hundred different sounds—and not just the songs of other birds. They imitate frogs, insects, cats, dogs, car horns, and even the beeps trucks make when they back up, though they make all these sounds not to mock anyone, but to attract mates and establish territory. The more songs they know, the more enticing they are to the opposite sex.

The mocking bird's repertoire is, in a sense, a composite of everything it's ever heard.

Finding a Voice

The same is true for poets.

Welsh poet Dylan Thomas (1914–1953) once worried that his poetry was too imitative of that of William Butler Yeats, one of his heroes. Nevertheless, while readers might catch an occasional hint of that influence, no one would ever mistake Thomas's poetry for Yeats's, so different are their voices and approach and imagery. Thomas was also captivated by Thomas Hardy, whose poetry he said he loved indiscriminately and in its entirety. And he also admired the French symbolists, even once jokingly referring to his younger self as "the Rimbaud of Cwmdonkin Drive,"[2] the road in Swansea, Wales, where Thomas grew up. And he loved Shakespeare, Milton, Robert Graves, Edith Sitwell, W. H. Davies, John Betjeman, and many others, and recordings are available of Thomas reading from their works. In fact, he said he preferred reciting the poems of other poets to his own.

Like the mocking bird, Thomas had a vast repertoire of voices that he loved, learned from, and sometimes mimicked, and in the aggregate, they blended until Thomas's poetic voice was unlike that of any other poet.

Think about your favorite poets. You would recognize their voices anywhere. Think of Whitman's conversational flash floods, his high-toned epistolary jazz riffs as in these lines, which make up section 18 of *Song of Myself*:

> With music strong I come, with my cornets and my drums,
> I play not marches for accepted victors only, I play marches
> for conquer'd and slain persons.
>
> Have you heard that it was good to gain the day?
> I also say it is good to fall, battles are lost in the same spirit
> in which they are won.
>
> I beat and pound for the dead,
> I blow through my embouchures my loudest and gayest for
> them.

Vivas to those who have fail'd
And to those whose war-vessels sank in the sea!
And to those themselves who sank in the sea!
And to all generals that lost engagements, and all overcome
heroes!
And the numberless unknown heroes equal to the greatest
heroes known![3]

Or consider the pinched, urbane, self-conscious interior monologues of T. S. Eliot, typified by these lines from "The Love Song of J. Alfred Prufrock":

And indeed there will be time
For the yellow smoke that slides along the street,
Rubbing its back upon the window-panes;
There will be time, there will be time
To prepare a face to meet the faces that you meet;
There will be time to murder and create,
And time for all the works and days of hands
That lift and drop a question on your plate;
Time for you and time for me,
And time yet for a hundred indecisions,
And for a hundred visions and revisions,
Before the taking of a toast and tea.[4]

Or think of Emily Dickinson's intensely compact exhalations with stunning images likely to erupt at any moment, as in the last two stanzas of "A narrow Fellow in the Grass" (a snake):

Several of Nature's People
I know, and they know me—
I feel for them a transport
Of Cordiality—

But never met this Fellow
Attended, or alone
Without a tighter breathing
And Zero at the Bone.[5]

No one writes quite like them. Their voices are as unique as fingerprints, so that you could pick them out of a police lineup by their writing style alone. ("Yes, officer, I would know Mr. Whitman's barbaric yawp anywhere.")

But each one got to that point by reading. Whitman deliberately echoed the cadences of the biblical Psalms; Eliot learned much of his technique from the French Symbolists; Dickinson was influenced by Ralph Waldo Emerson and Elizabeth Barrett Browning, among others. These poets read widely and indiscriminately.

Like these poets, our process must be that of the mocking bird. We have to admire, read, learn from, and sometimes imitate the work of many poets to figure out what our own voice sounds like.

Sounding Like Yourself

The first secret to finding your voice is patience.

I was tempted to make this chapter on voice the first one in this book, because, in a sense, it's the most important. Your writing voice is what defines you; it's who you are. But that voice only develops over time, after you've pondered and absorbed all the other lessons in this book.

The longer you write—and read—the closer you come to approaching a voice that wells up from inside you, from someplace genuine and visceral. A few rare poets, like Rimbaud, seem to have been born fully formed, with unique voices (like the full-grown Dionysus from Zeus's thigh), but one look at the juvenile writing of most poets—John Milton, John Keats, T. S. Eliot, Dylan Thomas, to name just four—reveals how much they learned about poetry, and about themselves, over time.

The second secret is the capacity for honest self-assessment. You need to listen to your poems before, while, and after you write them, constantly hearing what is working well and what is simply a reliance on the same old formulas you've used for years. You have to recognize when you're just marking time or *trying* to sound poetic. You need to get outside your poem and, in a sense, outside yourself, to read it with alien eyes. Be critical.

Be forewarned, though, that such self-assessment leads to a perennial dissatisfaction with your writing. And it should. You'll feel that you're never honing your words quite sharply enough—though that is actually a sign that you are maturing as a poet. As French poet Paul Valéry (1871–1945) said, "A poem is never finished, only abandoned."[6] That's okay.

Third, just as an opera singer exercises by doing scales, you too need to exercise your voice, by which I mean actual vocalization. Not only should you speak your own poetry aloud even as you write it (I like to walk alone at night, composing aloud), but you should also read the poems of your favorite poets aloud, just as Dylan Thomas loved to do.

What's more, you should memorize the poems you love—whether others' poems or your own. I can't tell you how many times I've been called upon to recite one of my poems from memory at some gathering. You should strive for as large a spoken repertoire as you can remember. Recite while you are driving. Fall asleep reciting silently to yourself. As the anonymous fourteenth-century Welsh *Red Book of Hergest* states: "Three things enrich the poet: myths, poetic power, and a store of ancient verse."[7] Nothing will enrich your poetry as much as letting your favorite poets' lines roll off your tongue.

Finally, imitate. It's okay. You will naturally tend to pick up the vocal habits—what jazz musicians call "the licks"—of the poets you most love. If you love only one or two poets, though, the danger is that you'll end up sounding like them, which is why it's important to love a host of poets and read them all. Like the mocking bird, listen to everything.

You Are Your Voice

I'm speaking from experience when I say, "You are your voice." For a period of six months, after surgery for throat cancer, I was virtually without a voice. I could communicate in a hoarse whisper but could not be heard in any but the quietest places and at close quarters. Other people ordered my food for me in restaurants.

The most interesting part was the psychological toll. My personality changed. I was frustrated much of the time, even angry when I couldn't be understood. I dwelt in a state of communicative claustrophobia, living daily with that common nightmare of wanting to scream but being unable to.

Our lives take these sudden turns from time to time. Everything shifts, and then we have to reassess, to ask ourselves who we really are in this new reality. I found myself falling back on the *other* voices in my life, voices that have been with me since childhood: my writing and a half dozen musical instruments became my new way of speaking. I got a lot of writing done and, in fact, wrote much of this book during that time.

Recently, another surgery restored my voice, which made me realize how much of *me* was entwined with my ability to speak. To my surprise, I discovered that we find our voice in order to find out who we are and not the other way around. It's a lifelong, dynamic process. Our voice, like our personalities, keeps changing.

So here is my advice for anyone wanting to write poetry:

Read widely.
Listen sensitively.
Write out loud.
Then let your voice emerge. It will speak for itself.

Exercises

- Ask yourself: Do I read poetry every day? Can I name ten poets whose voices have shaped me and informed my writing? Do I know them so well that I could write a pastiche of their style? Is my voice distinctive enough that a reader could distinguish it from other contemporary poets?
- How would you define your voice? Write a list of adjectives that both define your writing style as it is and as you'd like it to become. Perhaps even write a poem listing some metaphors that define the sound you want for your poetry.
- *Poem Assignment:* Pick out one of your favorite poets, contemporary or classic, and write a pastiche of their voice. Write it so precisely that you might even be able to fool someone.

Reading

Helpful Resources

- American poet Sandford Lyne (b. 1945) has written a very helpful book for new poets: *Writing Poetry from the Inside Out: Finding Your Voice through the Craft of Poetry* (2007).
- A wonderful resource for hearing classic poets read their own verse is Elise Paschen and Rebekah Presson Mosby's book-and-three-CD set *Poetry Speaks: Hear Great Poets Read Their Work from Tennyson to Plath.* (Yes, there are actually wax cylinder recordings of Tennyson

reading his poetry: "Into the valley of Death / Rode the six hundred …")

Classic Poets

- Dylan Thomas had one of the most unique and identifiable voices in twentieth-century poetry. Find a copy of *The Poems of Dylan Thomas* (2004) or, better yet, find recordings of him reading not only his own poems aloud, but those of his favorite poets. The best collection is *Dylan Thomas: The Caedmon CD Collection* (2004).

Contemporary Poets

- A friend once said that modern poetry is best when it approaches stand-up comedy. With this in mind, check out these CD recordings of American poet Billy Collins reading his poetry: *The Best Cigarette* (2011) and *Billy Collins Live* (2005).
- To learn more about slam performance, be sure to find *The Spoken Word Revolution: Slam, Hip Hop and the Poetry of a New Generation* compiled by slam poet Mark Eleveld. The book is informative and contains an audio CD.

Part Three: Mysterious Barricades

> The strategy to be deployed against the devil of acedia can be summarized in the phrase: joyful perseverance.
>
> —Jean-Charles Nault (b. 1970)[1]

14 Writer's Block: Sleeping with Bears

Do you ever feel like this:

> Unhappily I cannot produce anything at all, not only the luxuries like poetry, but the duties almost of my profession.… All impulse fails me: I can give no sufficient reason for going on. Nothing comes: I am a eunuch.

I find it encouraging that priest and poet Gerard Manley Hopkins (1844–1889), whose words those are, also had his dry spells—especially when I consider that within months after expressing those thoughts in a letter to his friend (and poet) Robert Bridges in 1888, Hopkins wrote some of his greatest poems: "That Nature Is a Heraclitean Fire," "St. Alphonsus Rodriguez," and "Thou Art Indeed Just, Lord." In that last poem, a sonnet, he even reclaims that slightly embarrassing word *eunuch* as he reflects on the creative desert he's just crossed. He calls himself "Time's eunuch" in the poem because he could "not breed one work that wakes," and in the final line he prays to God,

"Send my roots rain"[2]—a good prayer for any writer confronting writer's block.

At some point or other, most writers express frustration with a periodic inability to write. Poetry is, if nothing else, not easy. If it were easy, teachers of MFA programs would have to find other work. Wallace Stevens (1879–1955) once put it this way in a letter to his fiancée: "I shudder at Art.... [T]here is a great sleepy jumble in me seeking to be arranged, to be set in order."[3] Or consider this from Romantic poet John Keats (1795–1821): "I look back upon the last month, and find nothing to write about; indeed, I do not recollect one thing particular in it. It's all alike; we keep on breathing."[4]

Everybody has down times, sure, but these quotes have something else in common—something that seemed at first to be coincidence but I now realize is a fiendish conspiracy of chronology. Each of those poets wrote those lines in winter, which you will recall that François Villon called "the dead season."

The Doldrums

As I saw this pattern of midwinter dullness emerge, I began to fling myself at every volume of literary letters and journals I could find, and I soon discovered that, with many notable exceptions, January through March tend to be lousy months for writers. Our souls have a tendency to tromp off to a cave somewhere to hibernate with the bears, while our muses are happily sunning themselves on the beach in Bimini, having left us here with rattling furnaces and heavy socks.

All this may have something to do with Seasonal Affective Disorder (SAD), a common affliction for writers. Combine the worst months for colds and flus with the shortened days, the dreary skies, the lowered levels of vitamins D and C and calcium—all of which are regulated by the sun—and you have a recipe for "no sufficient reason for going on," as Hopkins says.

Of course, there's something just a bit self-indulgent about moping over one's lack of creativity, as if we're tempting someone, sooner or later, to smack us metaphorically and say, "Shut up and get back to work," which is probably why all of the above confessions were reserved for private diaries or letters to trusted friends (though Bridges epistolarily smacked Hopkins from time to time).

Consider two further cases. In January and February of 1915, Czech fiction writer Franz Kafka (1883–1924) experienced one of the worst creative crises of his life. He nearly gave up entirely—well before committing most of his greatest works to paper. Consider these extracts from his diary:

> January 4. Great desire to begin another story; didn't yield to it. It is all pointless....
>
> January 20. The end of writing....
>
> January 29. Again tried to write, virtually useless.
>
> January 30. The old incapacity....
>
> February 7. Complete standstill....
>
> February 25. [My life must] end unavailingly, be consumed in incessant doubt, creative only in its self-torment.[5]

The second case is not only cheerier but more instructive, largely because it doesn't come from the writer himself. William Wordsworth's ever-faithful sister, Dorothy Wordsworth (1771–1855), kept a valuable record of the poet's daily routines, and she was especially candid about his mid-winter incapacity of 1802. Throughout the months of January and February, he spent much of his time polishing, to his constant dissatisfaction, one particularly long narrative poem called "The Pedlar." It wasn't going well; he would work himself into a frenzy, collapse, then retire to his bed feeling ill:

> January 26. Wm wrote out part of his poem … and so made himself ill …
>
> February 1. Wm slept badly … worked hard at *The Pedlar*, and tired himself …
>
> February 3. Wm tired and did not compose …
>
> February 5. Wm not well …
>
> February 6. Wm slept badly …
>
> February 7. Wm had a bad night and was working at his poem. We sat by the fire and did not walk, but read *The Pedlar*, thinking it done, but lo! Though Wm could find fault with no one part of it, it was uninteresting, and must be altered. Poor William! …
>
> February 9. He fell to work and made himself unwell
>
> February 10. Wm sadly tired and working still at *The Pedlar* …

And on it goes, day after day, in that vein for the rest of February.

But here's the good news:

> March 26. A beautiful morning. William wrote to Annette, then worked at "The Cuckoo." … While I was getting into bed, he wrote "The Rainbow."
>
> March 27. A divine morning. At breakfast Wm wrote part of an ode. Mr. Olliff sent the dung and Wm went to work in the garden. We sat all day in the orchard.[6]

The poem "The Rainbow" is, in fact, the famous "My heart leaps up when I behold …," and the "ode" to which Dorothy Wordsworth refers is none other than "Ode: Intimations of

Immortality: From Recollections of Early Childhood." Think of it. Writing two of the most famous poems in the English language within twenty-four hours of each other! And what joy it must have been to go outside after that, pitch the dung, and then sit in the orchard for the rest of the day. He must have positively glowed.

And yes, *Wm* did finally complete "The Pedlar"—but not until two years later.

The Rules

So how do these examples of writer's block help—especially since none of us are Wordsworth, nor can we expect to write two immortal poems in one day?

Well, the model, as third-century Chinese writer Lu Chi says of the ax handle, is at hand. I returned to many of these same writers to glean a few rules for surviving the hibernation—until Mr. Olliff sends to us too a good wagon-load of dung to pitch in our gardens. These are the rules:

1. **Refocus on God.** French Benedictine monk Jean-Charles Nault (b. 1970) defines such times of dullness as "a sort of blockage, a break in the search for God."[7] When you are feeling unproductive, when, like Hopkins, all impulse fails you, then spend time in prayer. I love this beautiful, humble, nonsectarian prayer by Oglala Lakota poet Layli Long Soldier: "Whatever it is out there that's bigger than I am, that energy, can you help me out? Just help me out this evening as I sit down, and let's see what we can do. I'm willing to be helped."[8] Or just spend time in silence, being present with God without any expectations at all.

2. **Administrate.** How did Wordsworth spend his uncreative months? Polishing old poems, copying them, and sending them off to friends and publishers. So did

Keats and so did Hopkins. Forgive the guilt throwing, but how many poems have you sent off to magazines this winter? A dear poet friend of mine even made it her New Year's resolution to have three packets of poems out at magazines at all times. If a poem gets rejected, turn it around and send it back out there.

3. **Practice Inscape.** Hopkins coined a term—*inscape*—to describe how he approached his poetry. Although scholars argue about its precise meaning, to me it means this: get outside, observe, pull Nature into yourself, *into* your own soul. William and Dorothy took long rambling walks through the snow together and pitched dung in the garden. Kafka strolled through the barren winter gardens of Prague—and get this, he even went sledding! (Though he confessed that he had a mortal fear of getting hurt.) So do it. Get outside—even in the cold. Find the continuity between the frigid landscape outside and your own frozen creativity within—if for no other reason than to encourage that continuity to persist until the inner and outer weathers turn milder. Practice *inscape* so that you can experience the inevitability of spring inside yourself.

4. **"Keep on breathing."** Which means, I believe, take care of your health. When Keats wrote that phrase he was already experiencing the first symptoms of the tuberculosis that killed him the following year. I appreciate my friend Rev. Craig Moro, who recently reminded me to resist my propensity to think of my body as twenty years younger than it is. Many people who write have a tendency to skip meals, forget to exercise, and stay up too late reading, writing, revising, perpetually assuming they can get by on one less hour of sleep. Maybe two. That may work in the milder

months, but in the winter, it's downright dangerous. So give yourself a break. Work at your poetry, but don't overtax yourself.

5. **Play at the Edges.** When you are in the midst of a creative winter, get outside and play in the snow. Try some of these jump-starters when poetic cabin fever sets in:

- *Translate.* If you know a second language, start translating. Classic poets are always good to begin with, but if publishing is your goal, seek out contemporary foreign poets; many journals are eager to hear what new voices from other cultures are saying—with Amazon and other online booksellers, it's easy to find foreign books of poems. And translation can be an excellent way to transition you back into your own poetry. It's important to let those poets in your second language influence you as well.
- *Mistranslate.* Find a poem in a language you *don't* know, then pretend to translate it into English by looking for cognates—words that look or sound vaguely like English words—and stringing them together in resonant ways. For me, Dutch is always good because it can look a little like English, but I have no idea what it means. It's a silly exercise, but sometimes a few ideas for your own poems might occur to you.
- *Erase.* Find an old book, magazine, or newspaper you no longer want and don't mind marking up. Select any word from the first page to serve as the first word of a poem. Then, with a pencil, strike through as many words as you need to until you find an intriguing word to follow that first word. Then continue striking out words until you have strung enough words together

to make a poem. This is called erasure, or reduction, poetry.

- *Explore "found poetry."* Read through any old book of prose, the more obscure, the better, and find passages that can be broken into lines of poetry. For example, in Leonardo da Vinci's notebooks I found the following "found poem," which I turned into a haiku and later incorporated into a longer poem: "The earth is shifted / from its orbit by a wren / lighting on a branch."[9] W. B. Yeats, James Laughlin, and William Carlos Williams, Annie Dillard, Lewis Turco, among others, experimented with found poems.
- *Versify:* try writing light verse or experiment with humorous forms like the limerick or the epigram.

6. **Shut Up and Get Back to Work.** Austrian poet Rainer Maria Rilke (1875–1926) said that if you find yourself lacking for subjects for poetry, the fault is not in the world but in yourself. Harsh words, especially from someone who had more than his share of incredibly dry spells, but there's wisdom there too. Somewhere William Stafford, in his gentler way, simply says: Sit down, be still, observe what's around you, then write a line. Then, write the line that comes after that. And the next one. And so on. It may sound silly, but Stafford's Muse seldom found time for vacations that way.

Patience and Hope

Rest assured that spring—whether actual spring or the metaphorical one—will return. Your creativity *needs* to sleep with the bears from time to time. But it won't last forever. Where I live, just south of the 45th parallel, it is late February right now, and the geese have begun to return. The snow that has covered the ground without a break since last November is beginning to melt (giving a whole new meaning to François Villon's famous question "Where are the snows of yesteryear?" The answer is: They're still here!) The skunks are out of their dens—and on the warmer mornings the crows are starting to make a ruckus (probably chasing the overwintering owls away from their nests). The doves are cooing, the redwings are squawking, and the woodpeckers are making the woods near our house sound like a drum band at Mardi Gras.

And suddenly, I feel like writing a poem.

So give it time. In the cycle of the creative seasons, spring is always just around the corner.

Exercises

- Gather all your completed poems together. Make a list of all the ones that you think are good enough to send out to magazines and divide them into packets of three to five poems each. Then research which magazines you want to send them to. (See chapter 18, "Submission: Send That Stuff Out," for advice on packets and how to send poems to magazines.)
- *Poem assignment*: Try this as a mistranslation exercise: assuming you don't know Dutch, study this line from the verse play *Lucifer* by classic Dutch poet Joost van den Vondel (1587–1679): "En liever de eerste vorst in eenig lager hof / Dan in 't gezaligd licht de tweede, of nog een minder." Now, try to guess what the words might mean if translated into English. Now add your own lines to it to make sense of whatever you came up with.[10]
- *Another poem assignment*: Try a "found poem" experiment by picking up a copy of any old book of

prose. Obscure novels are often good, as are antiquated textbooks or the writings of Victorian naturalists. Anything old and unusual will work. Now, scan the book looking for poetic lines or even paragraphs hidden within the prose. Break the passage into lines and add stanza breaks if necessary. Play with line lengths and positioning on the page.

Reading

Helpful Resources

- Eric Maisel is my favorite go-to person when it comes to issues of creativity and writer's block. (I recommend a couple of his books in chapter 4 on "Process: The Empty Page.") I especially like his *Deep Writing: 7 Principles That Bring Ideas to Life* (1999).
- I found David Bayles and Ted Orland's *Art and Fear: Observations on the Perils (and Rewards) of Artmaking* (1993) to be unusually helpful in overcoming anxieties about creating. Although not specifically about poetry, the book offers lots of advice for artistic people in general.

Classic Poets

- This would be a good time to reread any of the classic poets mentioned in this chapter: William Wordsworth, John Keats, Gerard Manley Hopkins—all of whom are available in many editions in most anthologies of poetry in English.

Contemporary Poets

- For an intriguing erasure poems, find *Radi os* (2005) by Ronald Johnson (1935–1998), which is constructed from Milton's *Paradise Lost*, and *Newspaper Blackout* (2010) by Austin Kleon (b. 1983).
- Pulitzer-Prize-winner Annie Dillard (b. 1945) assembled a memorable collection of found poems, *Mornings Like This* (1995), which contains nearly forty poems that she found and reshaped, with no alteration other than line breaks and adding titles. Poet Lewis Turco (b. 1934) compiled an intriguing volume of poems partly found and partly inspired by Robert Burton's *The Anatomy of Melancholy.* Turco's book is called *The Compleat Melancholick* (1985).

Don't think. Thinking is the enemy of creativity. It's self-conscious, and anything self-conscious is lousy.
—Ray Bradbury (1920–2012)[1]

15

Self-Consciousness: Everyday Ecstasies

There's one in every family. A well-meaning retired uncle or a dear bright-eyed aunt who, at the worst possible moment, manages to quash the high spirits during those all-too-rare family gatherings by tossing out the leaden question "Aren't we having fun?" The room grows quiet. Self-consciousness wafts into the corners like stale Nag Champa.

In my case it took a slightly darker turn when a kindly uncle told me with great earnestness as I set off for college: "Enjoy your college years, Bob, they'll be the *best* years of your life," after which a sort of frantic terror possessed me, anticipating the precipitous downhill slide after graduation.

I used to work in a flower nursery—and loved the velvety, carmine scent of the roses. The smells in that greenhouse were exotic and rich, sweet enough to rot teeth. But that same summer, a country-western song hit the pop charts that advised the listener to "Stop and Smell the Roses" along the way.[2] As platitudes go, it's innocuous, but it made me think: Has it *ever* prompted *anyone* to do it? I had my doubts. What's worse, it ruined rose-smelling for me. I could not lean toward a newly opened bud without that song coming to mind. It was the scent of self-consciousness.

Perhaps you know this story from Leo Tolstoy's childhood—the one about the green stick. His older brother claimed to have discovered the secret to life—the key to unlocking the mystery of existence—and the brother had written it on a green stick, which he buried in the forest. Anyone finding the stick would "enjoy great happiness and make all mankind happy by the power of love."[3] When the child Leo begged his brother to tell him where the stick was buried, the brother said he would tell him on one condition: if Leo could stand in the corner and *not* think of a white bear. Of course, it's impossible. To prove that you're not thinking of a white bear is to be thinking of a white bear. Leo never found the stick.

The Inner Uncle

For me, this kind of self-consciousness is different from the anxiety I feel when confronting the empty page or experiencing times of drought, but it can be just as much of an obstacle. Sometimes, in the midst of the writing, I hear this voice that sort of croons, "Oh, that was a good line! Do that again" or "Don't mess this up if you're expecting a good poem in the end." After which I pretty much freeze. I have pages and pages of sketches that end abruptly with my most resonant lines.

Many writers tell you to pay no attention to your "inner critic," which is excellent advice and well worth heeding. But I find I don't so much have an inner critic as an inner uncle who says, "My, aren't we poetic today?"

The question is, how do you finish such poems? How do you *not* think of a white bear?

If this is not a problem for you (and I know many poets who toss off poems like an oak sheds acorns), then simply skip to the next chapter. But if you struggle with this form of writer's block, then here's a short list of coping strategies I have used over the years:

1. Befriend the Bear

Consider the possibility that the white bear may actually be a friend. Not cuddly like a teddy bear, and bigger than a Zuni fetish, but not a man-eater either.

I suspect that Tolstoy's brother's secret isn't buried in the forest at all. It's buried in the mind that is able to be aware of the mind-being-aware. That overripe awareness of "the self-perceiving-the-self" is one of the traits that separates us from the rest of the animal kingdom, as far as we know. It's what makes us human. A philosopher friend of mine even goes so far as to suggest that this multi-reflective inner mirror is, in itself, what we think of as the soul.

A fly's self-awareness is limited, and even a dolphin, which is supposed to have a modicum of self-awareness, could care less about the "secret of life." So neither of them writes poetry. Only an overripe, self-aware human mind could come up with Yeats's line "Like a long-legged fly upon the stream / his mind moves upon silence."[4]

My hunch is that if the green stick did, in fact, exist, here's what Tolstoy's brother would have written on it: "The white bear *is* the secret." Self-consciousness is much closer to self-awareness than we realize—and the distance between the two is relatively small. Perhaps Tolstoy's brother was teaching Leo a valuable, if subtle, lesson: that the struggle to overcome our debilitating inner confusions is often the first step toward creating art.

To see this in practice, read the Zen poets. The haiku poets, for instance, by striving for a kind of selflessness in their poems, arrive at self-awareness. Why else would they have written as if they themselves were absent? They were masters at not allowing an overripe self-consciousness to inhibit their living fully in the present. Their self-awareness enriches their every moment. Consider the great Japanese poet Masaoka Shiki (1867–1902) when he was gravely ill and searching his brain for a winter haiku. How long did he ponder before he finally wrote:

All I'm able to think of
is me lying here in this house
and snow everywhere[5]

It's a chilly, sad poem. It makes you shiver. But Shiki is a master of befriending the white bear, taking both the physical and the psychological stone walls that block his way and reaching ghost-hands through them to retrieve something beautiful and real. It's a poem about being in too much pain to write a poem.

2. Practice Everyday Ecstasies

Self-consciousness is a gift. Without it, we would probably miss all those small, little-noticed mysteries that occur almost every waking moment. Everyday ecstasies are all around us. How can any human ever be bored in a life so rich and varied?

Smelling the rose is a good example of an everyday ecstasy. But the trick is to do it with enough focus and patience so that the debilitating kind of self-consciousness simply fades into the distance. The next time you see a rose, try actually smelling it long enough to allow that stupid smell-the-roses song to drift into the back of the mind. It may not disappear, but it can be diminished.

But here's the scary part. If left to meditate long enough on that scent, you just might get a whiff of something that feels more like "fear and trembling" than "sweetness and light." Negotiating the terrain between those extremes is what much of the poetry of Rainer Maria Rilke (1875–1926) is about (at least as much of it as I understand). To really smell the rose, to let your senses open to all that lies behind and beyond and above it, is a spooky thing. You reach the point where you feel an eerie strangeness, a weird but fascinating sort of alienation. Where does the scent really come from? In this vast array of stars and galaxies, how did the smell of that rose at that moment even stand a chance of bursting into existence in the first place? How did we humans ever obtain the necessary equipment to perceive it?

Whether you believe the rose was formed by a wild cosmic Creator, as we Christians do, or by a vast cosmic void—either way—the soil from which it grows is vast and unfathomable. Beauty, when deeply apprehended, is not so much a "joy forever," as John Keats said, as it is a jolt to the central nervous system. Capture just a piece of that sensation, describe it vividly, and put it in a corner of a poem. Don't even worry about making sense—because that's what ecstasy is all about, perceiving something that goes beyond words, the almost said, as Juan Ramón Jiménez wrote. Never hesitate to listen to your inner mystic.

And by *everyday ecstasies* I mean every day. As we said before, make your writing a habit. Set aside an appropriate time and be satisfied with page upon page of humdrum observations if that's all you can muster. But do it. Remember what William Stafford said about low standards. Fiction writer Flannery O'Connor somewhere wrote that she believed in inspiration, but that she had to spend time each day writing so that she'd be ready whenever it decided to hit her upside the head. Noticing the everyday ecstasies is not a hard once you get in the habit, but it's easy to forget to jot down your thoughts about those experiences.

3. Practice Mindfulness

Mindfulness is a trendy word, but it's an age-old method of relaxing your brain, and it offers the surprising benefits of calming you, minimizing anxiety, refreshing the mind, and contributing to greater alertness and creativity. If every coin has two sides, the flip side of self-consciousness is mindfulness.

Different techniques exist, but this is the one I find helpful. I sit or lie in a relaxed position, with my eyes shut and away from any possible distractions like a phone or other electronic devices. Then I relax the muscles all over my body, actually focusing on my face, neck, and shoulders, which is where I tend to carry much of my tension, and I especially become aware of the tension behind my eyes because when I concentrate on something, I have a tendency to tighten up my eye sockets.

When everything is relaxed, I try to eliminate all words and images from my mind. If a random thought skitters into view, I simply imagine myself pushing it gently to the side. I allow the mind to go blank. Some people focus on their breathing, in and out. Many Christians, like myself, focus on being silent and relaxed in the comfort that God is surrounding them. It is, in fact, the technique that Christian contemplatives have practiced for centuries.

That's it. No revelations; no sudden insights. Just a spa-like relaxation for the soul. If for only five minutes, it can make you feel revitalized and more aware of everything around you.

4. Forget Poetry

Often, we do poetry best when we think about it least. To quote Thomas Merton once again, what he once said of contemplatives is every bit as true for poets: "Perhaps the best way to become a contemplative would be to desire with all one's heart to be anything but a contemplative."[6]

Some poets love poetry for its own sake; they love the idea of poetry, the romance and the emotional power of it. I felt that as a child when I first heard a really good poem read aloud to me by a good reader—when my mother, a drama major in college, read "My Last Duchess" by Robert Browning (1812–1889) to me.

But there are other poets who just love. They've learned that the point of poetry isn't poetry at all, but people. It's about relationships, communion with the reader. All poetry, ultimately, is a gift waiting to be given, which I think is what the Japanese Zen Buddhist poet Ryokan Taigu (1758–1831) was getting at in his famous poem:

> Why do people tell me my poems are poems?
> My poems aren't poems.
> Only when you realize my poems aren't poems
> can we really begin to talk about poems.[7]

The gift at the heart of a poem is not the poem but the alive, glowing, ecstatic awareness contained in it. The bottom line: Don't be poetic; be human. Just *be* and keep writing.

5. Practice Averted Vision

Sometimes the best approach to finishing a poem is to focus on something else. Pianist Walter Gieseking, in his book *Piano Technique*,[8] advises young pianists, after thoroughly memorizing a piece of music, to focus not on the technique—that is, the fingering, the notes, or the phrasings, all of which is now part of muscle memory—but to focus on the emotion. The pianist distracts himself of herself from the mechanics by concentrating on the delivery, by focusing on the listener.

It is essential to know the mechanics of poetry (your rhythms and rhymes, your line lengths and line breaks, the music your words make) so well that they become second nature; then you are freed to focus on the emotion behind the words.

Having Fun

It's a weird thing—this being alive. This breathing, thinking self. This river of blood flowing in circles through the veins. This mind that goes click click click as thoughts take shape out of some blank inner mist. As a child, I had a recurring nighttime dream of who I was—of what my soul was—a sort of disembodied, hyper-perceiving head, floating through a black, cold, starlit galaxy. I would turn my head slowly from side to side, glancing at the passing stars, hearing the high wind in my ears, and all the world below me. I was like the star child at the end of the Stanley Kubrick's film *2001: A Space Odyssey*.

Today, I have the same picture in my head. Except I am no longer adrift in the vast emptiness of space. Rather, I catch glimpses of color and shapes, people and trees and soaring birds and shuffling creatures; I catch the scents of roses and the endless forests in which powerful mysteries are veiled. The real world. The floating world. The world of wonders.

So now, if someone were to ask me, "Aren't we having fun?" I would respond, "Who could ever have imagined it would be like this? Yes, I'm having fun. I'm having more than fun."

And the white bear is having fun as well.

Exercises

- Find something you love to smell, like flowers, vanilla, bacon, whatever. Then sit in a chair and focus on it. You will probably find that after about forty-five seconds, you'll grow bored, other thoughts will intrude, you'll feel self-conscious and ask, "Why am I doing this?" But persist. Keep focusing on the smell. Then be aware of the tiny thoughts that keep intruding, and for each one ask these two questions: "Why did that thought occur to me?" and "Does it have any connection to the thing I'm smelling right now?" Somewhere in there, you may discover the seed for a poem.
- *Poem Assignment:* Like Shiki, write a poem about that feeling of being unable to write poems at times. What metaphors can you use to describe that?

Reading

Helpful Resources

- One recent book that is well worth reading about the themes in this chapter is *The Naked Now: Learning to See as the Mystics See* (2009) by Franciscan friar and priest Richard Rohr (b. 1943). Read especially his chapter "Three Ways to View a Sunset." He has many books about opening one's eyes to spiritual reality.

- I recommend Joy Kenward's book *The Joy of Mindful Writing: Notes to Inspire Creative Awareness* (Leaping Hare Press, 2017). It is an accessible introduction to mindfulness, filled with helpful tips and writing prompts.
- Distracted times always provide an opportunity to revisit the work of your favorite poets. Go back to them and read them with new eyes. They can be like poetic comfort food.

The office of poetry is not to make us think accurately, but feel truly.
—Frederick William Robertson (1815–1853)[1]

16

Depression: Many Unhappy Returns

The age-old notion that writers, to write, must be depressed goes at least as far back as Aristotle, who wrote, "Why is it that all those who have excelled in philosophy, statesmanship, poetry, and the arts are melancholic?"[2] English scholar Robert Burton (1577–1640), who wrote an entire book, *The Anatomy of Melancholy*, to anatomize his depression, put it more harshly: "All poets are mad."[3]

It's hard to name a famous poet who hasn't struggled with at least an occasional depression. By researching the lives of a thousand twentieth-century poets, psychiatrist Arnold Ludwig discovered that 77 percent had experienced at least one serious bout of depression, compared to 55 percent for fiction writers, and 46 percent for composers.[4] The phenomenon of poets being more depressed than other artists has even been given a name; sadly, it's called the Sylvia Plath Effect, and further research even suggests that female poets experience bouts of depression at a higher rate than their male counterparts.

Many noted poets have been hospitalized for depression—among others, William Cowper (1731–1800), Christopher Smart (1722–1771), John Clare (1793–1864), Gérard de Nerval (1808–1855), John Berryman (1914–1972), and Anne Sexton (1928–1974). Not even writers of humorous verse are immune to low periods. Master limericist Edward Lear (1812–1888), author of the beloved children's poem "The Owl and the Pussy Cat," lived in daily fear that his own epilepsy was somehow linked to creeping insanity.

So am I recommending depression as a path to poetry?

Of course not. But it remains an occupational hazard for even the most cheerful poets—sometimes especially for them. All this makes sense when you consider the realities that dedicated poets live with: the intentional confrontations with uncomfortable truths, the deep silences, the hyperactive sensual awareness, and the devastating creative droughts. And poets seem to be especially prone to debilitating self-doubt, perhaps because they engage in an activity that is ignored or dismissed as frivolous by a large portion of society.

I wish I could say that this chapter offers solutions. It doesn't. If you recognize the symptoms of depression in yourself, then it is essential that you talk to your doctor, seek professional counseling, and join a support group. Any depression, whether severe or mild, should be taken seriously.

But this chapter does discuss some resources that might help some creative people create in spite of, and perhaps because of, their depression.

The Midnight Disease

If you've ever sensed there might be an intimate connection between your depression and your creativity, then you should meet Dr. Alice W. Flaherty. As a professor of medicine at Harvard, a doctor of neurology, and perhaps most helpful of all, an excellent writer, Dr. Flaherty herself has faced serious clinical depression.

As both a medical researcher and a memoirist, she is in a unique position to outline the processes by which various psychological dysfunctions both hinder and aid creativity. The results of her research are gathered in *The Midnight Disease: The Drive to Write: Writer's Block, and the Creative Brain* (2004), a book that doesn't necessarily solve our problems, but it enlightens us as to what, neurologically, is going on in the brain at those times when we can't write—and at those times we can.

One of her more startling insights is that, according to scientific research, creativity is "more closely linked to mood instability than to cognitive traits such as high IQ."[5] In other words, "feelings," as blue or changeable as they may be, get us farther along the path to creativity than "thinking" does. Our emotions (which flow from the brain's limbic system) are more closely linked, neurologically, to the brain's center of creativity (the temporal lobes, just behind each ear) than they are to the center of reasoning and intellect (the frontal lobe). That's not to say that we should ignore the intellect, for it plays a major role in crafting and revision, but the intellect alone doesn't get us far. That close connection between the brain's emotional and creative centers is what has, for so long, given observers the impression that creative people are melancholic. But creative people often have a knack for turning their melancholy into art.

But this is not to say that we should cultivate depression. Rather, Flaherty's research suggests the opposite. Writers seldom write *while* they're at their lowest points. Instead, they tend to do their best work during their "up-swings," during their periods of improving moods. This idea allows us to redefine the experience of depression. Rather than seeing depression as the norm, we can view it as simply the temporary down time between bouts of creativity. The optimum—for creative pursuits, at least—is to have short, fairly mild depressions alternating with more extended upbeat moods. Flaherty's advice to artists: throw yourself into your work with renewed intensity once your feel your mood lifting.

We can see some of this cycle playing out in two very different poems by two very different poets who were roughly contemporary with each other.

John Keats: "Ode on Melancholy"

One of the most well-known poems in English about depression is "Ode on Melancholy" by English Romantic poet John Keats (1795–1821). In the first of its three stanzas, he gives the reader three bits of advice: (1) do not ignore your pain or try to deaden it with addictive drugs ("No, no, go not to Lethe, neither twist / Wolf's-bane, tight-rooted, for its poisonous wine"); (2) by all means resist the idea of suicide ("Nor suffer thy pale forehead to be kiss'd / By nightshade"); (3) and make an effort not to dwell on images of despair ("The beetle … the death-moth … / nor the downy owl.)" In sum, do not strive to "drown the wakeful anguish of the soul."

Rather, he recommends in the second stanza that "when the melancholy fit shall fall," you should

> … glut thy sorrow on a morning rose,
> Or on the rainbow of the salt sand-wave,
> Or on the wealth of globed peonies;
> Or if thy mistress some rich anger shows,
> Emprison her soft hand, and let her rave
> And feed deep, deep upon her peerless eyes.

In other words, he advises the depressed poet to seek out images of beauty, to return to the senses and the things of this world. He ends with the poet gazing eye-to-eye with a lover. This focus on Beauty and the senses is meant to stimulate the "upswing" that might restore your creativity and renew your spirits. While you might expect that this solution—that contemplation of beautiful things—is the cure for melancholy, it is not so simple.

In the third stanza, he reminds us of the uncomfortable truth that even "Beauty … must die." While this might seem to return us to a state of despair, he suggests another way of looking at Melancholy altogether. "In the very temple of Delight," says Keats, "veil'd Melancholy has her sovran shrine," alongside the other shrines in that temple, those of Joy and Pleasure. Although every worshiper must at some point pay homage to Melancholy, the worshiper remains in the temple of Delight all the while. Here Keats is describing the cycle of depression and the creative upswings when the dark mood starts to lighten.

Kobayashi Issa: "The Fly"

With much less complexity but every bit as much profundity, Japanese haiku poet Kobayashi Issa (1762–1828) suggests a similar process in this haiku about a fly:

> Don't kill that fly
> see, she is wringing her hands
> … and her feet[6]

You may wonder how this simple comic verse relates to Keats's complex ode. They seem to have little in common on the surface.

But the fact is that Issa lived a difficult and tragic life. As an infant, he lost his mother and was partly raised by a harsh and demanding stepmother. He experienced extreme bouts of depression as a teenager, which only made his life at home more difficult, and as an adult, he outlived two of his three wives and several of his children, even losing his house and all his possessions to fire. His haiku, many of which are humorous on first reading, must be understood in the context of the poet's personal tragedies. As one writer beautifully wrote, "Poetry and life were one in him. For Issa, a haiku was not the product of an exquisite fancy conjured up in a studio, but the vital expression of an actual life feeling. Poetry was a diary of his heart."[7]

In this haiku about the fly (one of ninety that he wrote about flies) Issa humorously points out flies' habit of rubbing their front and back legs together. In Issa's imagination, the fly is wringing her hands in fear of being killed, but a transformation takes place. The poet identifies so closely with the fly that they almost become one. In a sense, Issa is pleading with fate itself not to kill him. This is the low point of his depression. But by making the small joke about the fly wringing its back feet as well, he achieves the "upswing," the renewal of his energies and spirit. The lesson is similar to Hopkins's concept of inscape, of taking nature into one's own soul to find comfort.

Many Unhappy Returns

While I would never wish depression on anyone, it is not altogether inappropriate to wish you many unhappy returns, at least some small times of melancholy, so that you can find yourself coming out of them with renewed energy and creativity.

Experience both the melancholy and the delight, and find a place for them in your poems. As Keats concluded in his "Ode on Melancholy," only then can the writer's "strenuous tongue / … burst Joy's grape against his palate fine."

Exercises

- Read a selection of contemporary poets with an eye toward their expressions of melancholy or outright depression. Study how they approach those feelings and sensations.
- *Poem assignment:* Think about a period of depression you've experienced. Make a list of metaphors that attempt to capture the feeling of that time. Once you've done that, string some or all of those metaphors into a poem-story about that time.

Reading

Helpful Resources

- Psychotherapist Dr. Eric Maisel is one of the best writers on the subject of creativity and process. One of his most clarifying books on creativity and depression is *The Van Gogh Blues: The Creative Person's Path through Depression* (New World Library, 2002). In it, he redefines depression as a "crisis of meaning" and steps the reader through the process of finding new, more viable meanings.

Classic Poets

- While not *about* depression, the collection of prose poems by French poet Charles Baudelaire (1821–1867) called *Paris Spleen* (trans. Louise Varèse, 1970) arose out of the poet's attempt to deal with his own melancholy.
- One of the most interesting and tragic modern poets to analyze her depression in poetry was Sylvia Plath (1932–1963). Read *The Colossus and Other Poems* (1960), her only volume of poetry published in her lifetime, and *Ariel* (1965), published two years after her death.

Part Four: Finding Readers

I've arrived at a distinction: the appeal of light verse is to the intellect and the appeal of serious verse is to the emotions.

—Phyllis McGinley (1905–1978)[1]

17 Readership: Verse and Poetry

On May 10, 1953, Mother's Day, an eleven-year-old boy in the Upper Midwest gave his mother a sweet twelve-stanza poem, neatly rhymed. The final lines were:

> My dear mother, I hope that you
> Will never grow old and gray
> So that all the people in the world will say:
> "Hello, young lady, Happy Mother's Day."[2]

A decade later, that little boy was the most famous songwriter in the world—Bob Dylan. In spite of the millions of dollars in royalties he has earned since then, you don't have to think twice to bet that his mother, Beattie Zimmerman, before her death in 1999, wouldn't have traded that one poem for all the Tambourine Men in the world. She knew *real* poetry when she saw it.

Perhaps you remember when it was that easy. A finger-painting for your parents would elicit high praise and result in a Scotch-taped exhibition on the fridge. A poem for your grandmother would make her feel as though you'd just given her the deed to Xanadu complete with pink plastic flamingos in the yard. In my case, a set of clumpy clay ashtrays of my own creation were displayed in my parents' corner cabinet until the day they died.

The point of poetry is in the giving. We enact generosity every time we sit down to write a poem, giving ourselves to the imagined reader: our thoughts and emotions, our souls, our time, our attention.

Good for Whom?

I mention this because, when people hand me a poem to critique, they often ask, "Is it any good?" to which I usually respond, "Good for whom?"

A poem that you wrote for Mother's Day may be wrong for *The Kenyon Review* … but right for your mother. A poem worthy of publication in a literary magazine, by contrast, might be a complete embarrassment to your family, especially your mother. (What *would* William Blake's mother have thought if she had read this line by her son: "The grandest Poetry is Immoral.… the poet is Independent & Wicked."[3])

My own favorite poems are not the ones I've published, but the ones I've written for (and about) my daughters. They are not great poems, but they are momentous in their own intimate world. Since I suspect the following poem is not likely to be published elsewhere, I include it here by way of example. It's for my middle daughter, Molly, and it's called "Teacup":

> Such is the faith of four-year-olds
> that my daughter brought me
> a teacup with a missing handle
> and asked, "Can you fix this?"
>
> I took it from her hands
> and later placed it in a drawer

where other hopeless things are kept,
knowing that in a day or a year

she would forget about it completely—
unless she recalls (for such is my faith)
the helpless doting look in my eyes
when I said, "I'll see what I can do."

All I can do is hope that she will keep
faith in the face of hopeless things,
that she will someday turn to someone and say,
"My father was good at fixing things."

I suspect that when I'm long gone, those poems will have made a far deeper impression on the world—at least on three intelligent, deeply soulful women—than all the poems I'll have published (or not published).

The point is: poems are written for different readers, and it is important to know who they are and why you are writing to them.

Poetry and Verse

To come to grips with the different kinds of readers, it is helpful to come to grips with the different kinds of poems. In the Prologue, I mentioned that my Uncle John was a writer of *verse* rather than *poetry*. It's an age-old distinction but a useful one. Here are just a few of the kinds of verse that exist:

- *Occasional verse* is written to celebrate public "occasions," like weddings (a wedding poem is called an "epithalamion"), funerals (an "elegy" or a "dirge"), birthdays (I suppose you could call that "natal verse"), anniversaries, and, I suppose, ribbon-cutting ceremonies for strip-mall openings. Three US presidents,

Kennedy, Clinton, and Obama, commissioned poems for their inaugurations; most famously, Robert Frost (1874–1963) read a poem at Kennedy's in 1961.

- *Light, or humorous, verse.* Some poets, like Don Marquis (1878–1937), Dorothy Parker (1893–1967), Ogden Nash (1902–1971), and Phyllis McGinley (1905–1978) specialized in humorous verse, which is most often rhymed and metered for maximum comic effect. Lest anyone think lightly of light verse, McGinley won a Pulitzer Prize for hers in 1961 and was admired by such literary poets as W. H. Auden.
- *Children's verse.* Among the many poets who have specialized in writing verse for children over the centuries, Shel Silverstein (1930–1999) was one of the most influential in our time. Many esteemed literary poets have tried their hand at children's verse: T. S. Eliot (*Old Possum's Book of Practical Cats*), Gwendolyn Brooks (*Bronzeville Boys and Girls*), Richard Wilbur (*Opposites*), and many others.
- *Seasonal verse.* Like my Uncle John, writers of seasonal verse write primarily short pieces about flowers, the changing of the seasons, gardening, the weather, and the passage of time. This kind of verse is not necessarily trite or conventional, as many of the great Asian nature poets have proven. One contemporary example of exquisite seasonal verse is *Garden Time* (2017) by W. S. Merwin (b. 1927).
- *Religious, or devotional, verse.* Some of the greatest poems in English fall into this category and have been part of the literary canon for more than a thousand years. There are hagiographical poems (saints' lives), homiletic poems (short sermons), biblical paraphrases,

hymns, gnomic verse (bits of wisdom), charms and incantations, and more.

And this is to say nothing of *narrative verse* (stories), *declamatory verse* (speeches), *limericks*, *epitaphs*, *greeting card verse*, and more.

What separates the various forms of verse from poetry is not that verse is bad or awkward or somehow less legitimate. The difference, rather, is that verse usually has a clearly understood intention and a specified audience. Verse is poetry that has been enlisted to serve a secondary function; an epithalamion, for instance, expresses "best wishes" for the bride and groom; a riddle poem is for children; a hymn is for the congregation; and so on. Poetry, by contrast, is its own justification, an urgent soul-to-soul communiqué from the writer to whomever might happen upon the poem. Verse is like a polite letter sent to someone in the mail; poetry is a desperate message in a bottle thrown into the ocean and meant for whoever finds it.

But note: never should any serious poet disparage verse. In fact, most serious poets write it joyfully and artfully whenever the need arises. If you write poetry, don't be surprised if you are occasionally asked to write some lines for a friend's anniversary. I was once commissioned to write a short birthday verse to be read on the radio. While it is true that verse is sometimes poorly written, the same is true of poetry as well.

Devotional Verse

But we need to talk about devotional, or religious, verse.

Many people I meet at Christian conferences write poetry whose purpose is to communicate their deepest and most inexpressible religious feelings. This purposefulness places them in the long tradition of such poets as John Donne, George Herbert, John Milton, Thomas Traherne, the great hymn writers, and many more.

But other writers see poetry as an opportunity to convert readers to their faith, as a form of evangelization, even though the reality is that, second only to highway billboards perhaps, poetry is the worst medium for evangelization that exists. Such writers are akin to street-corner preachers, handing out tracts and shouting at passers-by. Writing bad verse about God is like asking the average person-on-the-street if he or she is saved; both activities are likely to garner the response "Don't know, don't care."

Poet (and friend) John Leax tells a story that makes this point. He once tried to explain to his daughter why he tried to "put Jesus" into his poems. It was, he said, so that readers might come to know Jesus and become Christians. His daughter replied, "Nope. It won't work. Nobody ever reads your poems."[4]

Evangelization is a face-to-face medium. It only succeeds when the relationship is two-way and when done in person. Poetry has a different purpose.

Rising Out of the Soul

So here's my theory about faith and poetry.

Although I'm a Christian, I don't try to write "Christian" poetry. Rather, I write about whatever I feel most deeply, my loves and hates, whatever in my heart is aching to be released, and then I simply trust that to the extent to which I am already covered by the Holy Spirit, my poetry will be covered by the Holy Spirit as well, no more, no less.

This seems wise to me. If we are Christians, whatever we write will also be Christian. But if we have an agenda other than exploring our own emotions, both the good and the bad, then we are not writing poetry but propaganda. For me, to insert even a smidgeon more piety into my writing than I actually possess is hypocrisy. The greatest witness to Truth is honesty—and such honesty encompasses my doubts, angers, bewilderment, passion and sometimes lack of passion, spontaneity, nuttiness, and the admission that I don't have the answer to every question. Honest poems ask questions, they don't answer them.

In his prophetic book, *Vanishing Grace* (2014), author Philip Yancey points out that Christians artists, along with activists and those whom he calls "pilgrims"—those who do not claim to know all the answers—are the only Christians who can still command even a small amount of respect in this radically post-Christian culture. The era of preaching in poems is over. Now is the time of coming alongside others by sharing our mutual griefs and joys and outrage and delight.

Theologian Francis Schaeffer once wrote, "To be a Christian tea-maker does not mean that we put a Bible verse on every bag; it means we make good tea."[5] We are called to make good poems, and we are judged not by our orthodoxy but by our truthfulness, craft, and imaginations. Poets like Thomas Traherne, William Blake, and W. H. Auden were Christians who happened to write brilliant poetry, but they were anything but orthodox. As paradoxical as it sounds, it is their very unorthodoxy that points to the Divine.

Exercises

- Lay out copies of all your best poems, and ask yourself, "Who was this one really written for? Who is most likely to enjoy it?"
- Do you write verse or poetry? When it come to the poets you love to read, which kind of poem do they write?
- *Poem assignment.* If you've never tried your hand at light verse, now is the time. Write about something funny that has happened to you or write about some ironic notion you've had.

Reading

Helpful Resources

- To see the best of both Christian verse and Christian poetry, find a copy of *The Oxford Book of Christian Verse* (1981), compiled by British poet Donald Davie (1922–1995).
- One of the finest books about balancing one's faith and one's art is *Walking on Water: Reflections on Faith and Art* (1981) by novelist Madeleine L'Engle (1918–2007).

To grow up is to accept vulnerability.

—Madeleine L'Engle (1918–2007)[1]

18

Submission: Send That Stuff Out

Once you've decided to send your poems to journals, whether in the general or Christian literary markets, the following tips may help. (Note: in this chapter, I use the terms *magazine* and *journal* interchangeably, though there are differences in format; for instance, magazines tend to carry advertising while most literary journals don't.)

First, a caveat: expect to get beaten up, stiffed, ignored, insulted, bruised, and verbally poked in the eye. It's called rejection, and every poet goes through it. Consider it a sort of hazing for initiates of an exclusive club only masochists would want to join. You find out quickly why the process is called "submission." (More about rejection in chapter 20.)

No less a poet than William Stafford (1914–1993) said he averaged five rejected poems for every published one—and that's *after* he became an established poet. That's an incredibly *good* average. Most experienced poets I know say they average about ten to twelve rejected poems for every hit. And I think they're shaving the numbers.

Although the process of submitting poems and facing the inevitable brush-off eleven out of twelve times is about as much fun as a kidney stone, you've got to do it. If you think your poems are good enough—as good as the poems you're reading in your favorite journals—then now's the time. *Send that stuff out!*

Here are the basics:

Research

The first rule is to *read*. Study the market and familiarize yourself with as many literary journals as you can. Study copies, whether in print or online, before submitting. Otherwise you might end up in a trashy-looking rag or sending the editors a completely inappropriate poem.

You can usually find an array of publications in university libraries, some public libraries, and even large bookstores. Or you can write the magazine for samples (most magazines will sell back issues online for a small fee). For additional ideas, here are some of the standard references for finding appropriate magazines.

- *Poet's Market* (Reader's Digest) is the most popular list of venues for publishing poetry. It is updated annually and contains heaps of valuable information. It is available at the larger bookstores and from Amazon. It's the best reference to start with. (In the next chapter, we'll look at *Poet's Market* in more detail.)
- *Directory of Poetry Publishers* (Dustbooks) offers the most comprehensive list. It is available only in digital form and must be ordered from the publisher directly: http://www.dustbooks.com. This is for the most serious of full-time poets.
- *Poets and Writers* magazine is targeted at writers trying to improve their writing and sell their work; it includes helpful articles, interviews, and information about contests, new journals, new publishers, calls

for submissions, etc. This one is worth subscribing to. Some of their content is also available online at http://www.pw.org.

- *NewPages:* this online reference lists literary magazines with links to their websites. Go to https://www.newpages.com/magazines/literary-magazines..
- For a listing of online journals, check *LitLine*: http://litline.org/links/onlinejournals.html or just search for "online literary journals." New ones appear every month.

A good way to find out about interesting magazines is to read the credits pages in the books of contemporary poetry that you're reading. Nearly always, there is a page on which the poet lists the names of the magazines that first published each poem in the book. If you write the kind of poetry that is in that book, then those magazines might be the ones you should start with, though, as mentioned before, review copies first.

Be sure to read the submission guidelines carefully for the magazine you're considering sending poems to. Most guidelines are available online, and it's important to follow them. Some magazines prefer email submissions; some prefer post; and some accept either. Some have very specific instructions on how the poems should be formatted—the typeface used, line spaces, margins, etc. Some magazines prefer "blind" submissions; that is, your name should not appear with the poem, though the titles of the poems should appear in your cover letter. Other magazines may ask for your name and address on every page. Just follow the rules set forth by the magazine. Be aware of any "reading windows," that is, those months during which the journal reviews poetry. A lot of university journals don't read during the summer, for instance.

As a general rule, don't submit to any site that charges you money—sometimes called a "reading fee." On the topic of scams, see *SFWA's Writer Beware Vanity Anthology information* (http://www.sfwa.org/other-resources/for-authors/writer-beware/) and *Wind Publications' Poetry Contest Caution site*: http://windpub.com/submitting.htm.

Print versus Online

Most people over the age of fifty assume that print journals are more prestigious than online journals. It's a thrill, as they say, "to see your name in print." But that overlooks one fact: when you get published in a print journal, it's a one-time shot. The magazine is issued and then sort of disappears down a rabbit hole when the next issue is released. The advantage of an online journal is that your poem will probably be archived and accessible for as long as the journal continues to have a website. When people search your name on Google, your poem will be one of the hits. So don't look down your nose at online publication even if you prefer print.

The Packet

Then you will compile your submission "packet"—either as paper copies sent in the mail or as an email with attachments.

The packet consists of the following pieces:

1. The Cover Letter, or Cover Email

Write a short message, no more than half a page, in which you introduce yourself and list the titles of the poems enclosed in your packet. Be businesslike and brief. Don't be cocky or cute, and don't apologize if you haven't published before. In fact, don't even mention it. If you have published, list two or three of your most impressive credits, but don't try to impress with a long vita or string of publications, and definitely don't try to explicate the poems to the editor. If the poems can't speak for themselves, then they're not speaking at all. And don't ask for comments or critical feedback.

Address the packet to the poetry editor by name (Mr. or Ms.) whenever possible. That is not a problem if you've reviewed a copy of the magazine in advance, or you can often find the name in the online submission guidelines.

2. The Poems

Send three to five short *unpublished* poems or two to three longish poems. Put your best one on top, and every poem should start on its own page. Unless otherwise directed in the submission guidelines, single-space the poems and double-space between stanzas, use a common typeface like Times New Roman or Courier (11- or 12-point type—nothing fancy or distracting) with one inch margins all around. For longer poems, put "stanza break" or "no break" in brackets in the lower right-hand corner whenever the poem flows onto the next page.

For paper submissions, use white or slightly off-white 8.5 x 11 paper (no pastels or grays). Put your name and address in the upper right-hand corner of each page, again unless otherwise directed. Don't staple the pages together. Use a small paper clip or leave them loose. Resist the temptation to spice up the cover letter or poems with doodles, cute notes, or outrageous typography.

3. Envelopes for Submissions (You'll Need Two)

I recommend that you purchase a box of 9 x 12 (#90) white or manila envelopes at the office-supply store. Into one of the envelopes you'll enclose your cover letter and your poems, unfolded, along with the second envelope (called the SASE—self-addressed stamped envelope). Alternatively, you can use two 6' x 9' (#55) envelopes with the cover letter and poems folded in half.

Address the SASE to yourself, and place the same amount of postage on that envelope as you put on the outside envelope. Fold it in half and place it beneath the poems in the packet. The magazine editor will use the SASE to return your poems in case of rejection. (One time a somewhat confused woman came back to me a few weeks after one of my workshops and indignantly told me that she had gone to several post offices, and none of them were able to supply her with SASEs. I explained to her that she needed to make them for herself—and provide the return postage.)

Keep a Submission Log

A log is essential: in either a notebook, digital file, or spreadsheet, keep an accurate, detailed "submission log," in which you record the title of every poem you sent in each packet, the date the packet was sent, and to which journal and editor. Record the response when it arrives and, if the poem is accepted, the promised date of publication and the kind of payment, if any, you will receive. This keeps you from sending the same poems to the same journal later, and the log will let you know how long you've been waiting for the magazine to respond.

Knowing the date of the publication also helps you know when to prompt the magazine if your accepted poem doesn't appear as promised. I've twice been accepted for publication only to have the magazines go out of business first.

Sometimes editors will write you an encouraging personal letter or insert a handwritten note on the form rejection letter, saying something like "Sorry these didn't meet our needs but please send more" or "Try again later." Keep track of any communications of that kind and record them in detail in your submissions log. Take that as an opportunity either to write that editor a personal thank-you or to send a few more poems that might work better for that journal. The key is not to let those contacts wither (but don't be overbearing or pushy either).

Simultaneous Submissions

Some magazines specify that they do not accept "simultaneous submissions," that is, they expect to be the only place to which you've sent those poems. If that is their policy, then abide by it.

The disadvantage for the poet is that, should the publisher reject your poems, you have to wait months in some cases before you can submit them to other magazines. Let's say, for instance, that you will have eight rejections before the poem gets published; if each magazine takes three months to respond, that means you'll wait two years. Most of us don't have that kind of time or patience.

Most journals understand—and even expect—that poets will submit the same poems to several magazines at once, and if they don't specify "no simultaneous submissions" in their guidelines, then take that as permission to submit to other magazines at the same time. If you do send your poems to several magazines simultaneously, though, the rule is that once a poem is accepted by one magazine, you need to notify the editors at the other magazines immediately, preferably by email, that you are withdrawing your submission. It's courtesy. Be polite, and thank the editors profusely.

The Wait

The most agonizing part is waiting. Some magazines will say in their guidelines how long to expect, usually about three months, though other magazines may take longer. Unless the publisher specifies a longer period, it is usually acceptable to send a short, polite (no complaining) query letter to the editor after three or four months, especially if they have a "no simultaneous submissions" policy. Alternatively, instead of querying the magazine, you would be justified in sending the same poems out to other magazines. Though remember, if one of the magazines accepts a poem, notify the others.

As in life, expect surprises. Don't be upset; just keep submitting.

The Rule of Three

Always have at least three packets of poems out at journals at any one time (that's a total of nine to fifteen poems in circulation, three to five in each packet). When one packet comes back rejected, look at the poems again, revise them if necessary, and send them back out as soon as possible—preferably before either of the other packets comes back. As in juggling, you should always keep at least two balls in the air at once.

Miscellaneous Advice

- *Never* pay to have your poems published. If the journal can't afford to pay you in cash (very few can), then they should at least compensate you by sending one or more "contributor's copies"—for free. Some will give you a free year's subscription.
- *Never* negotiate the payment. If all the publisher can offer you is a free copy of the magazine with your poem in it, be content with that. Even literary magazines that pay for poems don't offer more than about $25 for unknown poets. And "payment in copies" is the norm.
- Don't get suckered into the common publication scam in which the publisher accepts every poem they receive and makes the poets purchase a huge, expensive volume of bad poetry, sometimes as big as a phonebook, in which you need an index just to find your poem.
- Don't think about submitting your poems to a book publisher until you have a lot of credits in literary journals. A book publisher is going to want to see at least thirty to forty mature, highly polished poems, many of which have been published in notable literary journals.
- Submit to contests (listed in *Poets and Writers* and online) if you like, but don't count heavily on them. Your main focus should be journals. Many contests require a submission fee, which is okay as long as it's not too exorbitant. If you know the name of the judge,

study that person's poetry to get an idea of what kind of poem they might like. A Marxist street poet-judge will probably not be impressed by a villanelle.

****

Those are the basic rules. There are no guarantees, but persist. The process takes a fair amount of record keeping and patience, but it is more energizing than this brief outline suggests. And, if all goes well, it will all feel worthwhile when you receive those letters that begin, "You poem has been accepted ..."

Exercises

- Look through all your poems. Which ones are good enough to be sent out to the magazines you're familiar with? Try assembling them into packets of three to five poems.

Reading

Helpful Resources

- Two outstanding short introductions to poetry submissions are Helene Ciaravino's *How to Publish Your Poetry* (2001) and Thomas A. Williams's *Poet Power: The Complete Guide to Getting Your Poetry Published* (2002).

I have never met a person who has never written a poem.

—Judson Jerome[1]

19

Resources: A Trip through *Poet's Market*

I've thumbed through *Poet's Market* from time to time ever since I was a teenager—back when American poet Judson Jerome (1921–1991), that patron saint of the unpublished, was the general editor. But somehow I only kept half an eye on the details. Usually, as I flipped through the book's magazine entries, I sensed that the book had far more to offer than I was taking advantage of.

So, I recently decided to scan through all the entries in its main section, which contains information about magazine and book publishers who accept poetry submissions, as well as the contest section at the end. You wouldn't expect that reading through a hefty 480-page reference book would be dramatic, enlightening, and funny, but it was all those.

It was like an epic journey, and my itinerary was threefold:

- To jot marginal notes beside those magazines that sounded like good venues for my poetry. (Notes like:

"This one takes haiku," "This one accepts forms," "This one likes narratives," and so on.)

- To put a big X next to those magazines for which my poetry is totally inappropriate (there were a lot of those): *The Journal of the American Medical Association*, for instance, and horror/gothic magazines, like *Mythic Delirium*.
- Finally, to put a check mark beside those magazines I want to review actual copies of.

Here, then, are some of my observations from that journey.

Classy Rags Don't Brag

I was amused by the number of small (that is, tiny) magazines that consider themselves the last, lonely purveyors of literary quality to the Western world, magazines so discerning that they publish exclusively unrecognized geniuses. When you read the rest of their entry you often find that their average press run is about 100 copies, 10 of which are sent to subscribers, the rest handed out on the streets of San Francisco, Portland, or wherever. I remember one magazine years ago that puffed boldly that the kind of poetry it wanted was "surgical steel punk, arterial ink, ecstatic gremlins, and hysterical saints." Its press run? Three hundred (and I'll bet they were rounding up). I don't mean to belittle such magazines. I admire their idealism and energy, and I too have published in my share of idealistic "little" publications.

But good literary magazines seldom grandstand or feel the need to puff themselves up. *The Atlantic* states that it "publishes some of the most distinguished poetry in American literature" because it does. *The New Yorker* simply says, "A quality weekly magazine … for a literate audience." Most magazines, of course, fall somewhere in the vast territory between the extremes, but you can usually tell which ones are full of decent poetry and which are full of themselves.

To Every Poem There Is a Season

My guess is that about half of the magazines I was most interested in sending my poetry to were based at colleges and universities, which means that they read poetry only during the school year, while the student staff (mostly unpaid) is on campus. The most common window is September to May, but watch carefully for such variations as September-December (for those journals that only publish a winter issue), or January-March (for those that only publish a spring issue). Most academic literary magazines publish three to four issues per year, though most still indicate that they will not accept any submissions during the summer. As a result, you'll have to dig a little deeper into *Poet's Market* to find those (mostly non-academic) magazines that accept summer submissions.

Read before Submitting

Don't depend on *Poet's Market* alone. Although I admit I've occasionally sent poems to magazines that I've never read (as do most of the poets I know), you can save yourself a lot of angst, hair-pulling, and postage stamps by tracking down an issue or two of whatever magazine you've decided upon. Sometimes a trip to a university library does the trick. It's astonishing how many journals they will carry. If they don't carry the one you want, most magazines provide samples via mail or online, usually for a small fee.

The two main reasons to *read* the magazine first is to save time and embarrassment. For instance, I've submitted translations of 150-year-old French poetry to magazines that *only* publish contemporary translations. I once sent a mixed batch of sonnets and free-verse to a journal that said it "favors" traditional forms. Had I examined a copy first, I would have found that they publish exclusively traditional forms. And, what's even more embarrassing, I have sent mixed batches of fixed verse and free verse to magazines that stated no preference—but I later found only publish free verse, which, by the way, is still the predominant preference, despite a nearly a half century of Neo-Formalism.

Don't Let the Polemics Get You Down

Many journals have axes to grind—political, social, cultural. For instance, I was mistaken in thinking that the Neo-Formalist wars were over. They are raging as furiously as ever—at least if one judges from the pages of *Poet's Market*. In one corner, those who think rhyme, meter, and form can have a valid place in contemporary poetry, and in the other corner, those who equate those devices with fascism and neo-colonialism.

Many "-isms" can be found among the various magazine entries in *Poet's Market*. There are anarchist publications, Christian publications, feminist publications, neo-goth publications, and many more. So be alert to the cultural slant of the magazines you're considering.

Poet's Market Is Not Comprehensive

During your trip to the local university, you will discover a lot of great magazines that are not listed in the pages of *Poet's Market*—and not just literary magazines; many magazines of various faiths and denominations are not listed in *PM*, but they publish a fair amount of poetry. Remember to check our your local publications such as city magazines, entertainment guides, and arts calendars, many of which publish local poets.

For Christian poets, denominational newsletters and magazines often publish poetry by members.

Don't Pay Reading Fees

Some smaller magazines charge you a "reading fee," that is, a set price per submission, usually between one and five dollars. While everyone has to make up their own mind, my advice is to skip those magazines. They argue that such fees are necessary to keep the magazine afloat, which is a weak argument, when you think about it. It speaks to their limited circulation, for most magazines strive to at least break even with their subscriptions alone.

Check Out Specialty Magazines

I was stunned by the number of special-interest magazines that solicit poetry relating only to their interest. Here's just a small sampling: family, gay, Jewish, Buddhist, fantasy/sci-fi, sports, Tolkien, mental illness, medical, jazz, humor, cleaning business, dreams, travel, rural, prison life, migrant workers, photography, insects, disability, childbirth, nudism, volcanoes, science, and many more. I suspect that nearly everyone reading this has at one time or another written a poem about at least one of those topics. In my own translating, I have run across no less than four French poems about pipe-smoking, and to my amazement, I found a magazine dedicated to pipe smokers that solicits pipe-smoking poetry!

Tub-Thumpers Are Not Welcome

By far the most common phrase in *Poet's Market* is "does not want Hallmark verse." It's a code, really, for all that is saccharine and sentimental, sing-songy, and conventional, most of which comes badly packaged with forced rhymes and trite thoughts (which we discussed in chapter 12, "Rhyme, Meter, and Forms"). But it's a phrase worth taking to heart. Those few magazines that accept rhymed and metered verse are usually careful to specify: "Must be *awfully good* to be considered." Hallmarkers had better stick to, well … Hallmark.

****

Those are the souvenirs from my trip. It's a journey I encourage everyone reading this book to take. Do what I did: put notes in the margins beside those magazines and contests that sound like possible venues for your poetry; put an X next to those not worth your time (which will be the majority of them). And then start sending.

The annually updated edition of *Poet's Market* usually appears around the last week of September or the first week of October. That's perfect timing because fall is when the poetry submission season really kicks in—when all those university magazines start reading. My advice is to send early in the cycle (late August or September) in hopes of having responses by Christmas. Then, send out the rejects in a second round of submissions in January. With luck, you will have acceptances by April. If not, send out the remaining unpublished poems in May for the "summer" season. By September of next year, the new edition of *Poet's Market* will be out and you can start your process over once again.

You already write it—so take the chance. Get involved in the business of trying to have your poetry published. Send it out. And to make your submissions more strategic, read through *Poet's Market* carefully. Take it to the beach this summer in lieu of the latest novel. Do yourself a favor and invest in your poetry.

Exercises

- If you're serious about seeing your poetry in print, make your own trip through *Poet's Market*. It is updated every year. It is currently edited by American poet Robert Lee Brewer and published by Writer's Digest Books, Cincinnati, Ohio.

Poetry is not a career, but a mug's game. No honest poet can ever feel quite sure of the permanent value of what he has written.

—T. S. Eliot
(1888–1965)[1]

20
Rejection: A Prayer to Saint Rebuff

My first rejection letter was from *The New Yorker*.

I was in the eleventh grade. My English teacher, Mrs. Zillman, had assigned the magazine as our main text for the year. It was a brilliant idea. Everyone was to subscribe, and we were to read each issue and report on our favorite items month by month, short stories, articles, reviews, poetry. "Wouldn't it be cool," I thought, "if I could get a poem in the magazine before the year was up? Wouldn't *that* impress everyone?" It's hard to know which was worse—my arrogance or my ignorance.

No need to tell you how that story ended.

But I remember scrutinizing the poetry in those issues, trying to figure out what it took to get into *The New Yorker*. To this day, I can remember reading "The Dead Hive" by W. S. Merwin (b. 1927) with awe and fascination and gaining a sense of what the magazine was looking for. (This was back when poet Howard Moss [1922–1987] was the poetry editor.) Even then, I could see that they didn't want good poems or even great poems. They wanted poems with a sense of astonishment—sometimes subtle, sometimes pyrotechnic. But always catching you off guard. (See chapter 9, "Insight and Surprise.") The poems were never just competent. They were off-beat, off-the-wall, off-to-the-races. Like those huge upward-pointing floodlights in the parking lots of used-car dealerships at night—they lit up the sky at odd angles.

Among other memorable rejections slips is one I received in graduate school from the literary journal *Kayak* in the late 1970s. It was a full 8½-by-11 sheet, showing an old Victorian etching of a gentleman's gentleman bodily tossing an inebriated vagrant down the front steps of an exclusive London men's club—what used to be called "the bum's rush." The caption below it, as you can guess, read, "Thank you for your submission, but unfortunately it does not meet our current needs ..."

Let's face it. You're poets. I can't tell you anything about rejection you don't already know. You've read the "standard literature" in the various writers' guides and references, which usually includes the following advice:

- Learn what you can from each rejection. Ask yourself, "Why would the magazine have rejected this?"
- Remember: it's not a rejection of you, just your poem.
- It doesn't mean your poem's not good, it just means it didn't suit their publication.
- Treat rejections like medals you've earned in battle.
- Remember how many times Frost or Whitman or whoever was rejected before getting published.
- Remember that publishing doesn't really change your life or validate you as a person.
- "What doesn't kill you makes you stronger" (Nietzsche).

Good advice. But it still hurts.

So instead of the conventional advice, I thought I'd share a couple ideas I've never read in the standard literature.

Slips

First, I'm amused by the concept of having the rejection appear as a *slip*. My suspicion is that the size of the paper on which the rejection is printed is proportional to the publication's financial status. That is, profitable magazines send out rejection "letters"—8½ by 11, trifold—because they can afford the paper. Journals that send you a half-, third-, or even a quarter-sized "slips" are obviously pinching pennies. They can't afford stationery. Those that only send postcard rejections are scraping the bottom.

Call it sour grapes, but I've consoled myself at times with this thought: "If they can't afford stationery, then obviously not many people even *want* to read their stinking magazine." If I receive a full-size rejection "letter," then I can console myself with, "Well, at least I tried and was rejected by the best."

Either way, I feel better.

Conflagrations

I wonder if we could devise some sort of nonsectarian rite involving rejection slips—like snipping them into small pieces and scattering them upon the waters of the River Lethe, the mythological river of forgetfulness. Or perhaps just eviscerating them with a butcher knife would be more appropriate. I wonder if the ashes of burned rejection letters might not have prophetic powers—like tea leaves or the entrails of sacrificial animals.

Now that I come to think of it, the idea of burning rejection letters makes me ask an essential question: Why do I keep them in the first place? Is it an act of egocentricity? Do I keep them because I hope someday to shake them in the faces of the rejecting editors and say, "See, you were *wrong*!" Do I keep them because I have an overinflated concept of my talent? Are the letters simply a testimony to my misunderstood genius?

No, I don't think so.

Two or three times in my younger days, when a girlfriend transitioned into a *former* girlfriend, I ritually burned her letters. There was something satisfying and cathartic about it—especially if she had rejected me before I had the chance to reject her. So if I had no qualms about burning personal letters, why do I save rejection slips?

I'm beginning to think that saving them may even be part of the problem. Whenever we feel we have to prove ourselves to somebody (like a rejecting editor), it means that we are really trying to prove it to ourselves. Keeping the letters is not arrogance or delusion so much as it's insecurity.

So I propose this: collect all your rejections slips into one neat pile every year. Then, sometime in April, that is, during National Poetry Month (and possibly even April Fool's Day), offer up your stack for your own miniature sacrificial bonfire. Spring is the perfect time—the Rites of Spring. Burn them. Put them behind you. Send them up as incense to the same nasty little deities who, for some reason, also like the smell of those old incinerated love letters. Those old gods have the time for such nonsense. But the point is, *you* don't—you should be working on new poems.

And the second point is that you should try to have as many rejections slip when every April rolls around as possible, not because you want the fire to burn longer, but because that means you've sent out a lot of poems this year. And with that many poems going out, you may have managed to get some published.

A Few Coping Strategies

Of course, in spite of the bonfire or the numbers of poems you did manage to get published, rejection will always happen. So here are some positive coping strategies.

First, *send up*. Yes, yes, I know the conventional dictum—send a poem out to the best magazines first, then work your way down the ladder until you find a lower-rung magazine that takes it. You sort of let the poem meet its level of inferiority.

But what's curious to me is that once in a great while the exact opposite works. If you sincerely believe that your rejected poem is good—and is genuinely publishable—then maybe you just sent it to the wrong magazine. Try sending it to a slightly better magazine the next time around. The key, though, is that you know in your gut it's good.

I remember a cycle of seven Christmas poems I wrote years ago. Year after year, I sent them to very small devotional magazines—and I was continually rejected. It baffled me. Finally, I decided to send it to a larger, national magazine with a sizable circulation—and strangely, they not only accepted it, they illustrated each of the seven poems and paid me $150—the most I've ever been paid for a single poem!

If sending up doesn't work for a time or two, then revert to the standard operating procedure of sending down—or perhaps laterally.

Second, *send smart.* When a poem is rejected, it's easy for panic to set in—causing you to take the scattershot approach to publishing. You're tempted to sit down with *Poet's Market* and send the poems out to anyone who might be even vaguely interested. You start sowing your grain a little too broadly.

Nothing can replace an actual visit to your local university library or possibly an evening spent online, just to browse among the magazines that publish poetry. First, you'll find a *lot* of magazines that aren't listed in *Poet's Market.* Second, you'll get a sense for what kinds of poems they're publishing. I'm embarrassed by how far astray some of the descriptions in *Poet's Market* have led me because I didn't look at the actual magazine first. (As I mentioned in the previous chapter, I sent some of my translations of nineteenth-century French poetry to a magazine that claimed to specialize in French translation—only to find, when looking at an actual copy, that they only publish translations of *contemporary* French poetry—a fact not mentioned in *Poet's Market*).

Ever had an embarrassing rejection letter that said, "We're sorry, but our magazine publishes according to given themes each issue, and your poem just didn't fit into any of our forthcoming themes"? A brief glance at their website or an actual copy of the magazine would have clarified that point beforehand. They'll usually tell you what the themes of future issues will be.

Third, *send often*. You know what they say in Chicago around election time—"Vote early; vote often." Do the same with your poetry. Don't let the dust settle on a rejected poem. Get it back in the mail. Remember the "Rule of Three" in chapter 18. If it makes you feel better, make a small improvement or two, change a comma or a line break, just to give yourself the illusion that it's now a better poem. But get it back in the mail.

A Small Story

One time I saw a gentleman, perhaps in his seventies, slip and fall on the ice. He wasn't hurt, thank goodness, and as I helped him to his feet, he said, "Thank God. That's one less time I'll have to fall." I wrote a poem about that incident.[2]

I now think of that man as my "patron saint of rejection." I call him Saint Rebuff. I remember him whenever I receive a rejection letter, and I say, "That's one less rejection I'll have to receive."

People often ask: "How do I get my poems published?" The answer is: persist. There's no shortcut or magic formula. Just keep trying.

So, next April, make a little bonfire and throw the ashes to the wind.

And as you do, say a little prayer to Saint Rebuff.

Exercises

- If you have received rejection slips in the past, what have you done with them? Are they still in the bottom of a drawer somewhere? Make a plan for them rather than letting them sit there.
- *Poem assignment.* Write a poem in the form of a spoof rejection letter, explaining to the poet all the reasons your fictional magazine cannot publish that person's poem.

Reading

Helpful Resources

- To encourage and amuse you, find a copy of *Pushcart's Complete Rotten Reviews and Rejections: A History of Insult, A Solace to Writers* (1998) edited by André Bernard and Bill Henderson.

"Well, Robert, and what are you writing now?" he was asked.
"Poetry," said Robert.
"Oh dear," said his acquaintance. "There is no money in poetry."
"No," replied Robert with conviction; "but there is no poetry in money."

—Robert Graves (1895–1985)[1]

21 DIY: Self-Publishing

You wait. For some inexplicable reason, the journals persist in rejecting your poems and book publishers don't seem interested. As you keep working, a sort of funk sets in, and you wonder if it's all worth it. Self-doubt breeds depression, and the whole thing seems to spiral. At this juncture, you might be tempted to chuck the whole idea and, in the words of novelist John Kennedy Toole, "go out to a movie and get more out of life."[2]

But the hopeful message is this: you're not helpless. You have options—and not just *good* options but *empowering* ones.

Network

Poets have a species-wide reputation for being notorious introverts—which means, according to psychotherapist M. Scott Peck, their vital juices are restored more by being alone than by being with others.[3] Which is perfectly okay, by the way. Think of Emily Dickinson.

But if you're having a hard time finding an audience for your poetry—the right readership—then you may need to seek out a small community of like-minded writers and artists, even if it's just two or three people. That is the creative cluster you will trust to guide you in your search for readers. Let them advise you about the best markets for your poems. Let them share their wisdom and experience with you as you share yours with them.

The first step is to network. Most communities have writers' groups, but if yours doesn't, then that's your cue to start one of your own. Other writers will not only critique your work to improve it, but they will suggest venues for publication. As a collective, the writers' group is invested in helping every member find outlets for their work.

Also, search online for "writers conferences" and consider attending, especially if they are in your geographic area. It's a good way to meet not only writers but editors. Most such conferences offer lectures, workshops, critique sessions, and valuable information.

Finally, support your local arts organizations in general by attending exhibitions, concerts, plays, and festivals. No matter where you live, you're likely not the only struggling artist within a short driving distance, so it can be an encouragement to talk with others and even develop synergy between the arts. I've done poetry readings accompanied by jazz musicians, and a poet friend of mine once wrote poems to accompany pieces in a photography exhibition.

Poetry Readings

In 1996, President Clinton officially designated April as National Poetry Month, and since then, nearly every bookstore, library, and college worth its salt sponsors some sort of poetry event, often readings and book signings, throughout that month. Major poets are sometimes invited to read, but most often the event is organized by and for local poets as an outlet for their work.

If your community doesn't sponsor poetry readings, then again, organize your own event for yourself and other local poets.

You may be surprised how receptive bookstores and libraries and even churches might be, although it will help if you can show them that you are able to bring in an audience. Attendance is crucial. You will need to extend personal invitations to friends, church members, and family, and ideally, you will draw the largest crowd by having several poets read their work. That way, each poet draws his or her own group of acquaintances to the event, so that one poet's guests are thereby exposed to the other poets as well.

But you don't have to wait till April. These events occur throughout the year in most medium-to-large-size cities, but the key is to attend as many such events as possible. When major poets come to read at your local library or college, find a seat in the front row. If a writers' group sponsors a reading by local writers, attend and get to know as many people's names as possible, which may even lead to your being invited to read at similar events in the future. Coffee shops sometimes sponsor "open mic" poetry nights. Get there early and sign up. Or organize your own event.

Then there are poetry slams. If you're intrigued by the phenomenon, then search for "poetry slam" on YouTube, but far better is to attend a local slam to check out the atmosphere, the style of poetry presented, and the idiosyncratic rules. Slams combine intense oral poetry with high-energy performance, and the audience provides an immediate response. The response, by the way, can be either positive or negative, so it can be a daunting experience for some poets.

The point of reading aloud is that poetry has to exist "in the ear" as well as "in the eye." Public reading not only gets your poems heard, it helps you network with other writers and artists in your area. This is one area of life in which introverts need to come out of their shells.

Broadsides

The simplest way to get a poem into the hands of readers is to print it out on a sheet of paper. No surprise there. It's called a broadside. It may feel as if all you're doing is running your poem through the computer printer, and you're right. Anyone can do that, so what makes that special?

What makes it special is when you put as much artistic consideration into the presentation of that poem as you put into the poem itself. The challenge becomes an aesthetic one—to make your poem look as beautiful (or as wild or as revolutionary or as intriguing or as shocking) as possible. The form must fit the content.

There is a long literary tradition of making such single-sheet poems into works of art, using elegant papers (sometimes handmade), beautiful typefaces (though readable), and visual elements like typographic designs or illustrations. To get an idea of the possibilities, go to Google and search "broadside poems," and then click "images." You will encounter an array of beautifully presented poems, from the cheaply produced to the dazzlingly creative.

I've seen broadside poems passed out at weddings and funerals and memorial services and Sunday-morning worship. I've seen poets pass out such broadsides as a thank-you to those who attended their poetry readings. They are a good way to promote your book (or chapbook or print-on-demand book) or just to give as gifts for your family and friends.

If you know an artist, ask if they'd consider designing your poem's presentation. Talk to your local independent print shop about specialty papers; they usually have a small stack of fancy deckle-edge handmade papers stashed away in a cabinet somewhere. Printers usually *love* these kinds of projects as a much-needed break from the corporate brochures and wedding invitations they're used to printing. You might be surprised how inexpensive a run of fifty or a hundred broadsides might be.

Alternatively, it's amazing how creative some poets can be with simply their home computer and a modicum of decorative taste. Hunt around at your local stationery shop or office-supply store for interesting papers. Perhaps decorative rubber stamping can be added. Your only constraint is your imagination. Broadsides needn't be complicated or overdone, but it is up to you to make them appealing and powerful.

Unfortunately, unless your broadside is a work of art worth framing in its own right, you will not be able to sell them. So the point is to give them away. The joy is in giving and, most importantly, getting your poem in the hands of readers.

Chapbooks

One of my favorite activities is to conduct workshops at conferences and writers' festivals on how to make chapbooks. I love to see the attendees' eyes light up when they realize that they can take control of the publishing process themselves by making their own small books relatively cheaply and giving them to friends, family, and those who attend their poetry readings.

A chapbook, if you've never seen one, is basically a simple booklet in which a number of printed pages are stacked together, then folded and fastened along the spine with staples or thread. Usually, a chapbook is no longer than forty-eight pages, since most staplers (find what's called a "saddle stapler") can't penetrate more than about twelve sheets of paper. (Each sheet of paper, when folded, has four pages.) But that allows for a lot of poems when you think about it. Again, go to Google and type in "poetry chapbooks," and then "images." As with the broadsides, you'll be amazed at the variety and creativity some poets and publishers have brought to this simplest of all book forms.

The chapbook has a long history in English literature; the early tales of Jack the Giant Killer (of Jack and the Beanstalk fame) were printed in chapbook form, and major contemporary poets like Robert Bly (b. 1926) and Diane di Prima (b. 1934) are often published by high-quality chapbook presses. Typographer and printer Allan Kornblum (1949–2014) was a driving force in the book-arts movement in the US and founded two publishing enterprises that issued gorgeous hand-printed chapbooks:

Toothpaste Press and Coffee House Press. His books are exquisite. (Again, Google "Coffee House Press" / "Images.")

Although most poetry chapbooks are hard to sell and usually don't get printed in editions of more than a few dozen copies, that's better than not seeing your work in print at all.

Print-on-Demand

For longer books, consider print-on-demand (POD). These are perfect-bound (paperback) books that are printed inexpensively on elaborate book-making machines. Independent printers have popped up all around the country that will print copies of authors' books for a fee. You'll find them listed online; search for "print-on-demand printers."

While traditional publishers print in bulk to save costs (that is, the larger the print run, the lower the cost for each book), POD books, by contrast, are printed one at a time as needed. They are self-published by the author through one of those POD printing establishments. Our local bookstore, Schuler Books in Grand Rapids, Michigan, has its own print-on-demand kiosk machine and has published hundreds of authors' titles.

As with chapbooks and broadsides, you, as the author, are responsible for preparing the look and layout of the interior as well as the cover. The two most common criticisms of POD books are that the print quality can look less polished than traditional printed books, and the covers often look amateurish. Despite rumors to the contrary, books *are* judged by their covers. It's a fact of life.

If you are considering self-publishing a few copies of your poetry book through the POD process, consider hiring a professional graphic artist to design the cover and possibly the interior as well. An artist is an added expense, but if you're serious about selling copies, then the more professional appearance is worth it, giving the book what the publishing industry calls "perceived value."

Contests

Although the odds of winning a poetry contest are even longer than getting a poem published in a magazine, it's sometimes worth the effort, especially if you think an individual poem neatly fits the profile of the contest. Check *Poets and Writers* magazine for the latest competitions. Although such contests are highly competitive, libraries and newspapers frequently sponsor poetry contests for local poets, and your chances greatly increase.

The Dinner Table

As anticlimactic as it may seem, your family and friends are, and always will be, your first, most immediate, most receptive, and most responsive audience, even if you are already publishing in magazines. Think of it this way: who else is more likely to respond to your poem the minute you finish it? Who else loves you even in your wildest moments?

When you publish a poem in a magazine, no one is likely to write you a fan letter, and by the next issue, most readers will have forgotten your name. When you publish a volume of poems, you are unlikely to be reviewed in the *New York Times Book Review*. As American humorist Don Marquis (1878–1937) once famously said, "Publishing a book of poetry is like dropping a rose petal down the Grand Canyon and waiting for the echo."[4]

So your family and friends are your best chance to hear that echo—though in the natural order of things, your family is likely to give you easygoing praise while your friends will offer critical feedback. It's good to have both.

This book, then, ends where it began, with Uncle John reading to his family with his sunny smile and rhetorical flourish. Don't be shy about reading to your friends and family, even if it's at the dinner table at Easter. They won't think less of you. But even if they do, as Uncle John said, "Us dogs don't mind."

Exercises

- Of the poems you've written, select some of the best—then read them aloud.
- What is your Plan B? If it were to take five more years before you get a poem published, what do you plan to do in the meantime? Look at the alternatives to traditional publishing listed in this chapter. List them in the order that seems most amenable to your and your personality.
- *Poem assignment*. Write a poem that can be read aloud at high volume—as if for a poetry slam. Nothing too quiet or "interior." Make it bold and "out there." If you tend to write poems on the page, compose this poem out loud, and only write each line down when you feel you've gotten it just right.

Reading

Helpful Resources

- You can find any number of websites and books that will step you through the process of making chapbooks. You are also welcome to contact me for a copy of my whimsical but informative chapbook called *Making a Poetry Chapbook* (Perkipery Press, 2016).
- Austin Kleon's *Show Your Work: 10 Ways to Share Your Creativity and Get Discovered* (2012) suggests some great practical steps you can take now to get your work out there, even while you're waiting to be published.

- It's the romantic in me, but Eric Maisel's *A Writer's Paris: A Writer's Journey for the Creative Soul* (2005) is one of those books that make me *dream* big dreams about my writing. Maisel not only describes the benefits from actually going to Paris to write, but he helps you imagine a sort of inner-Paris so that you can tap that kind of bohemian creativity.

"Poetry is a verdict, not an occupation."

—Leonard Cohen (1934-2016)[1]

Epilogue
Come All You Comelings

You've probably sensed this already ... poets are different. Odd ducks. Black sheep. Out of step. Which is not to say they aren't sociable or don't live normal lives—or that they're better than other people, or worse. In fact, poets *are* other people, every-day, ordinary people, as we saw in chapter 1, "The Working Poet"—people who sit in cubicles, sell shoes and lattes, take the kids to ballet practice, and so on.

But when poets write well, they make people think ... or cry, or get excited, or grieve, or experience delight or bafflement or comfort, or get upset or even angry. Ray Bradbury once wrote that a writer should be "a thing of fevers and enthusiasms."[2] Good poets mess with our emotions, though that can make some people uncomfortable. A well-known poet I know even lost his job because of a poem he wrote. Poets, in that wonderful old English expression, run *widdershins*, counterclockwise, against the flow.

Some of them—the most prophetic—have even been perceived as threats to society. The Roman poet Ovid (43 BCE–18 CE) was exiled to the Black Sea for offending the emperor;

François Villon (1431–c. 1463) was banished from Paris; and poets as diverse as Richard Lovelace (1617–1657), Paul Verlaine (1844–1896), Oscar Wilde (1854–1900), Nâzim Hikmet (1902–1963), and, one of my favorites, William Wantling (1933–1974), to name but a few, spent time in prison for various scandalous reasons. The great Spanish poet Federico García Lorca (1898–1936) was assassinated by Francisco Franco's fascist death squads. And when the soldiers of Chilean dictator Augusto Pinochet came to search the house of Pablo Neruda (1904–1973) as the poet was dying, Neruda told them, "You won't find anything dangerous here, except poetry."[3]

Good poets don't rubber-stamp the status quo or stump for the powers that be, nor do they subscribe to the popular prejudices of their time. "Poetry," said Beat poet Allen Ginsberg (1926–1997), "is not an expression of the party line."[4] Victorian poet and critic Matthew Arnold (1822–1888) wrote that poetry is "the criticism of life."[5] The poet's job is, in a sense, to be an acute observer, an elegant dissenter, a discerning outsider—because from where else can you see the inside most clearly?

Think about the image of the Stranger on the Bus that we talked about in chapter 2. If you now find that you are

- dredging up odd thoughts and powerful feelings,
- courting the Muse and wooing Beauty,
- paying attention to the senses and reminding others of the worlds we have lost to complacency and neglect,
- confronting the lies and excesses in our culture and in our souls,
- and putting all those things into poems,
- then you yourself are now the Stranger on the Bus, making other people, I sincerely hope, uneasy.

In this, good poets of whatever faith follow in the footsteps of Jesus. According to the King James Bible, the apostle Peter says that followers of Jesus are "strangers and pilgrims"[6] in this world. Other translations use such words as "sojourners and exiles" (ESV), "foreigners" (NIV), and "aliens" (NASB). My favorite is John Wycliffe's rugged Middle English translation from the fourteenth century, in which he says we are "comelings and pilgrims." What a beautiful, rich, archaic word: *comeling*—a person who comes from somewhere else.

The fact is that we do come from somewhere else, and such is the estate of not only the poet but, truth be told, everyone who walks the earth. All of us, from the famous to the foolish, from billionaires to babies, are comelings and pilgrims, strangers and aliens, but we need poets because their job is to remind us.

I say all this as a way to wish you God's speed on your journey as a maker of poems. Expect to be out of step but accept that as the price of creativity. But write. With intensity and toughness. It is up to you now to do the work. No one else can do it for you.

And so, I offer this final benediction:

May you be comfortable with the uncomfortable
and attentive to the silence inside you.
May your senses embrace the world
and your loves and losses speak deeply.
May you be truthful, fear nothing, and love ferociously,
for that is the incalculable poetry of God.

I conjure you all who have had the evil luck to read
this ink-wasting toy of mine, even in the name
of the nine Muses, no more to scorn the sacred
mysteries of poesy; no more to laugh at the name
of poets, as though they were next inheritors to
fools; no more to jest at the reverent title of the
rhymer; but to believe … that whatsoever they write
proceeds of a divine fury.

-Sir Philip Sidney, *The Defence of Poesy* (1595)

Acknowledgments

Portions of this book first appeared between 2000 and 2004 at the website WorkingPOET.com and its associated email newsletter, and a few chapters were presented as talks at the Maranatha Christian Writers' Conference and the Calvin College Festival of Faith and Writing.

Sue Johnson, Brian Phipps, and Angela Scheff edited material for each issue of the WorkingPOET newsletter and contributed reviews, poems, and articles. Laura Blost designed the website and Deb Leiter helped edit the online content. Thanks to them for their friendship, contributions, and insights. And thank you to all the faithful readers and contributors to the monthly workshop newsletter.

Thank you to Kim Tanner of Kim Tanner Literary Services, who has once again proved invaluable in compiling the permissions for this book.

Thank you to Kelsey Kaemingk for editing an early draft of this book and helping to organize its basic structure.

Thank you to those who fueled my interest in poetry and writing early in my life: my mother, Barbara Anderson Hudson, and my father, George "Ray" Hudson, my great uncle John Henning Anderson, Robert Thomure, David Thomure†, Craig Moro, Robert Cramer, Dennis J. Kopaz†, Rebecca Schmidt, Marilyn Laslo, Michael Webster, Robert F. Gross, Thomas Farrell, and Robert Moore†.

Thank you to Tim Beals of Credo Communication for his tireless work and brilliant agenting, and to George and Karen Porter and the other bold folks at Bold Vision Books for taking on this project.

And finally, thanks to Shelley Townsend-Hudson, the best poet I know.

Bibliography

1. Helpful Books

Writing Poetry

Addonizio, Kim, and Dorianne Laux. *The Poet's Companion: A Guide to the Pleasures of Writing Poetry.* New York: Norton, 1997.

Behn, Robin, and Chase Twichell, eds. *The Practice of Poetry: Writing Exercises from Poets Who Teach.* New York: HarperPerennial, 1992.

Borges, Jorge Luis. *This Craft of Verse.* Cambridge, Mass.: Harvard Univ. Press, 2000.

Drury, John. *Creating Poetry.* Cincinnati: Writer's Digest, 1991.

Dunning, Stephen, and William Stafford. *Getting the Knack: 20 Poetry Writing Exercises.* Urbana, Ill.: National Council of Teachers, 1992.

Espy, Willard R. *Words to Rhyme With: A Rhyming Dictionary.* New York: Checkmark, 2006.

Ferlinghetti, Lawrence. *Poetry as Insurgent Art.* New York: New Directions, 2007.

———. *What Is Poetry?* Berkeley, Calif.: Creative Arts Book Company, 2000.

Hass, Robert. *A Little Book on Form: An Exploration into the Formal Imagination of Poetry.* New York: HarperCollins, 2017.

Hirsch, Edward. *A Poet's Glossary.* New York: Houghton Mifflin, 2014.

Hollander, John. *Rhyme's Reason: A Guide to English Verse.* New Haven, Conn.: Yale Univ. Press, 1989.

Hugo, Richard. *The Triggering Town: Lectures and Essays on Poetry and Writing*. New York: Norton, 1979.

Joselow, Beth Baruch. *Writing Without the Muse: Sixty Beginning Exercises for the Creative Writer.* Pasadena, Calif.: Story Line Press, 1999.

Kowit, Steve. *In the Palm of Your Hand: The Poet's Portable Workshop*. Gardner, Maine: Tilbury House, 1995.

Leax, John. *Grace Is Where I Live: The Landscape of Faith and Writing*. La Porte, Ind.: WordFarm, 2010.

Lyne, Sandford. *Writing Poetry from the Inside Out: Finding Your Voice through the Craft of Poetry.* Naperville, Ill.: Sourcebooks, 2007.

Maxwell, Glyn. *On Poetry.* Cambridge, Mass.: Harvard Univ. Press, 2013.

McDowell, Robert. *Poetry as a Spiritual Practice: Reading, Writing, and Using Poetry in Your Daily Rituals, Aspirations, and Intentions.* New York: Simon & Schuster, 2008.

Oliver, Mary. *A Poetry Handbook.* San Diego: Harcourt Brace & Co., 1994.

Skelton, Robin. *The Shapes of Our Singing: A Comprehensive Guide to Verse Forms and Meters from Around the World.* Spokane: Eastern Washington Univ. Press, 2002.

Skinner, Jeffrey. *The 6.5 Practices of Moderately Successful Poets: A Self-Help Memoir.* Louisville: Sarabande, 2012.

Stafford, William. *Writing the Australian Crawl: Views on the Writer's Vocation.* Ann Arbor: Univ. of Michigan Press, 1978.

Strand, Clark. *Seeds from a Birch Tree: Writing Haiku and the Spiritual Journey.* New York: Hyperion, 1997.

Whitworth, John. *Writing Poetry.* London: A. & C. Black, 2001.

Whyte, David. *The Heart Aroused: Poetry and the Preservation of the Soul in Corporate America.* New York: Doubleday, 1994.

Wooldridge, Susan G. *Poemcrazy: Freeing Your Life with Words.* New York: Clarkson Potter, 1996.

Wynne, Octavia. *Poetic Meter and Form.* New York: Bloomsbury, 2016.

General Writing

Aronie, Nancy Slonim. *Writing from the Heart: Tapping the Power of Your Inner Voice.* New York: Hyperion, 1998.

Barnstone, Tony, and Chou Pink, eds. *The Art of Writing: Teachings of the Chinese Masters.* Boston: Shambhala, 1996. Magnificent ancient wisdom on writing.

Bayles, David, and Ted Orland. *Art and Fear: Observations on the Perils (and Rewards) of Artmaking.* Santa Cruz, Calif.: Image Continuum, 1993.

Cameron, Julia. *The Artist's Way: A Spiritual Path to Higher Creativity, 25th Anniversary Edition.* New York: Tarcher, 2016.

———. *The Vein of Gold: A Journey to Your Creative Heart.* New York: Tarcher, 1997.

Deutsch, Laura. *Writing from the Senses: 59 Exercises to Ignite Creativity and Revitalize Your Writing.* Boston: Shambhala, 2014.

Goldberg, Bonni. *Beyond the Words: The Three Untapped Sources of Creative Fulfillment for Writers.* New York: Tarcher/Putnam, 2002.

———. *Room to Write: Daily Invitations to a Writer's Life.* Pasadena, Calif.: Tarcher/Putnam, 1996.

Goldberg, Natalie. *Writing Down the Bones: Freeing the Writer Within.* Boulder: Shambhala, 2005.

Hudson, Robert. *The Christian Writer's Manual of Style.* Grand Rapids, Mich.: Zondervan, 2016.

Hughes, Elaine Farris. *Writing from the Inner Self: Writing and Meditation Exercises That Free Your Creativity, Inspire Your Imagination and Help You Overcome Writer's Block.* New York: HarperPerennial, 1992.

Jiménez, Juan Ramón. *The Complete Perfectionist: A Poetics of Work.* Ed. Christopher Maurer. New York: Doubleday, 1997.

Kleon, Austin. *Show Your Work: 10 Ways to Share Your Creativity and Get Discovered.* New York: Workman Publishing, 2014.

———. *Steal Like an Artist: 10 Things Nobody Told You about Being Creative.* New York: Workman Publishing, 2012.

Klinkenborg, Verlyn. *Several Short Sentences about Writing.* New York: Knopf, 2012.

Maisel, Eric. *Deep Writing: 7 Principles That Bring Ideas to Life.* New York: Tarcher, 1999.

———. *Fearless Creating: A Step-by-Step Guide to Starting and Completing Your Work of Art.* New York: Tarcher/Putnam, 1995.

———. *The Van Gogh Blues: The Creative Person's Path through Depression.* Novato, Calif.: New World, 2012.

Plotnik, Arthur. *Spunk and Bite: A Writer's Guide to Punchier More Engaging Language and Style.* New York: Random House, 2005.

Royal, Brandon. *The Little Red Writing Book: 20 Powerful Principles of Structure, Style and Readability.* Cincinnati: Writer's Digest Book, 2004.

Shaughnessy, Susan. *Walking on Alligators: A Book of Meditations for Writers.* San Francisco: HarperSanFrancisco, 1993.

Ueland, Brenda. *If You Want to Write.* St. Paul: Schubert Club, 1984.

Wood, Monica. T*he Pocket Muse: Ideas and Inspirations for Writing.* Cincinnati: Writer's Digest, 2001.

Reading Poetry

Brett-Smith, H. F. B., ed. *Peacock's Four Ages of Poetry; Shelley's Defence of Poetry; Browning's Essay on Shelley.* Boston: Houghton Mifflin, 1921.

Gioia, Dana. *Can Poetry Matter? Essays on Poetry and American Culture.* Minneapolis: Graywolf, 1992.

Hirshfield, Jane. *Nine Gates: Entering the Mind of Poetry.* New York: HarperCollins, 1997.

Jarrell, Randall. *Poetry and the Age.* New York: Knopf, 1953.

Lerner, Ben. *The Hatred of Poetry.* New York: Farrar, Straus & Giroux, 2016.

Orr, David. *Beautiful and Pointless: A Guide to Modern Poetry.* New York: HarperCollins, 2011.

Pinsky, Robert. *Democracy, Culture and the Voice of Poetry.* Princeton, N.J.: Princeton Univ. Press, 2002.

Pound, Ezra. *ABC of Reading.* New York: New Directions, 1934.

Simon, John. *Dreamers of Dreams: Essays on Poets and Poetry.* Chicago: Ivan R. Dee, 2001.

Whitman, Walt. *An American Primer.* San Francisco: City Lights, 1970 [1904].

Anthologies

Appleton, George, ed. *The Oxford Book of Prayer.* New York: Oxford Univ. Press, 1985.

Bowman, Catherine, ed. *Word of Mouth: Poems Featured on NPR's All Things Considered.* New York: Vintage, 2003.

Causley, Charles, ed. *The Puffin Book of Magic Verse.* London: Puffin, 1974.

Collins, Billy, ed. *180 More: Extraordinary Poems for Every Day.* New York: Random House, 2005.

———, ed. *Poetry, 180: A Turning Back to Poetry.* New York: Random House, 2003.

Duffy, Carol Ann, ed. *Stopping for Death: Poems of Death and Loss.* Illus. Trisha Rafferty. New York: Henry Holt, 1996.

Dunning, Stephen, Edward Lueders, and Hugh Smith, eds. *Reflections on a Gift of a Watermelon Pickle and Other Modern Verse.* New York: Scott, Foresman, 1966.

Eleveld, Mark, ed. *The Spoken Word Revolution: Slam, Hip Hop and the Poetry of a New Generation.* Sourcebooks Media Fusion, 2005.

Ferlinghetti, Lawrence, ed. *City Lights Pocket Poet Anthology.* San Francisco: City Lights, 2015.

Hamill, Sam, ed. *The Erotic Spirit: An Anthology of Poems of Love, Sensuality, and Longing.* Boston: Shambhala, 1999.

Hass, Richard, ed. *The Essential Haiku: Versions of Basho, Buson, and Issa.* New York: Ecco, 1995.

Hirsch, Edward, ed. *Poet's Choice.* New York: Harcourt, 2006.

Housden, Roger, ed. *For Lovers of God Everywhere: Poems of the Christian Mystics.* Carlsbad, Calif.: Hay House, 2009.

———, ed. *Risking Everything: 110 Poems of Love and Revelation.* New York: Harmony, 2003.

———, ed. *Ten Poems to Change Your Life.* New York: Harmony, 2001.

———, ed. *Ten Poems to Set You Free.* New York: Harmony, 2003.

———, ed. *Twenty Poems to Bless Your Marriage.* Boston: Shambhala, 2012.

Keillor, Garrison, ed. *Good Poems.* New York: Penguin, 2002.

———, ed. *Good Poems for Hard Times.* New York: Penguin, 2005.

Majmudar, Amit, ed. *Resistance, Rebellion, Life: 50 Poems Now.* New York: Knopf, 2017.

Maltz, Wendy, ed. *Passionate Hearts: The Poetry of Sexual Love: An Anthology.* Novato, Calif.: New World Library, 1996.

Paschen, Elise, and Rebekah Presson Mosby, eds. *Poetry Speaks: Hear Great Poets Read Their Work from Tennyson to Plath.* Book and 3 CDs. Sourcebooks Media Fusion, 2001.

Strand, Mark, and Eavan Boland, eds. *The Making of a Poem: A Norton Anthology of Poetic Forms.* New York: Norton, 2001.

Young, Kevin, ed. *The Art of Losing: Poems of Grief and Healing.* New York: Bloomsbury, 2013.

Publishing Poetry

Bugeja, Michael J. *Poet's Guide: How to Publish and Perform Your Work.* Brownsville, Ore.: Story Line Press, 1995.

Ciaravino, Helene. *How to Publish Your Poetry.* Garden City Park, N.Y.: Square One, 2001.

Corey, Stephen, and Warren Slesinger, eds. *Spreading the Word: Editors on Poetry.* Beaufort, S.C.: Bench Press, 2001.

Hudson, Robert. *Making a Poetry Chapbook.* Ada, Mich.: Perkipery Press, 2016. (Available from the author at roberthudsonbooks.com.)

Williams, Thomas A. *Poet Power: The Complete Guide to Getting Your Poetry Published.* Boulder, Colo.: Sentient, 2002.

The Writer's Life

Glazner, Gary Mex. *How to Make a Living as a Poet.* Brooklyn: Soft Skull, 2005.

L'Engle, Madeleine. *Walking on Water: Reflections on Faith and Art.* Wheaton, Ill.: Shaw, 1981.

Maisel, Eric. *Living the Writer's Life: A Complete Self-Help Guide.* New York: Watson-Guptill, 1999.

———. *A Writer's Paris: A Writer's Journey for the Creative Soul.* Cincinnati: Writer's Digest, 2005.

Rohr, Richard. *The Naked Now: Learning to See as the Mystics See.* New York: Crossroad, 2009.

See, Carolyn. *Making a Literary Life: Advice for Writers and Other Dreamers.* New York: Random House, 2002.

2. Books of Poetry Referenced in This Book, With Some General Recommendations

Akiko, Yosano. *River of Stars: Selected Poems of Yosano Akiko.* Trans. Sam Hamill. Boston: Shambhala, 1997.

Basho, Matsuo. *Basho: The Complete Haiku.* Trans. Jane Reichhold. Tokyo: Kodansha, 2008.

———. *The Narrow Road to the Deep North and Other Travel Sketches.* Trans. Nobuyuki Yuasa. New York: Penguin, 1966.

Baudelaire, Charles. *The Flowers of Evil.* Trans. James N. McGowan. New York: Oxford Univ. Press, 2008.

———. *Paris Spleen.* Trans. Louise Varèse. New York: New Directions, 1970.

Berry, Wendell. *A Timbered Choir: The Sabbath Poems 1979–1997.* New York: Counterpoint, 1971.

———. *This Day: Collected and New Sabbath Poems.* Berkeley, Calif.: Counterpoint, 2013.

Berryman, John. *Dream Songs.* New York: Farrar, Straus and Giroux, 1969.

Blake, William. *Blake: Complete Writings.* Ed., Geoffrey Keynes. London: Oxford Univ. Press, 1972.

———. *Songs of Innocence and of Experience: Showing the Two Contrary States of the Human Soul.* Facsimile edition. London: Tate, 2007.

Blanding, Don. *Vagabond's House.* New York: Dodd, Mead & Co., 1928.

Brooks, Gwendolyn. *In the Mecca.* New York: Harper & Row, 1968.

Brown, George Mackay. *Poems: New and Selected.* New York: Harcourt Brace Jovanovich, 1971.

Collins, Billy. *The Best Cigarette.* Antonow Press, 2011.

———. *Billy Collins Live.* Random House Audio, 2005.

———. *The Rain in Portugal.* New York: Random House 2016.

———. *Sailing Alone around the Room: New and Selected Poems.* New York: Random House, 2001.

———. *The Trouble with Poetry.* New York: Random House, 2005.

Corso, Gregory. *The Happy Birthday of Death.* New York: New Directions, 1960.

Dickinson, Emily. *Emily Dickinson's Poems—As She Preserved Them.* Cambridge, Mass.: Harvard Univ. Press, 2016.

Dove, Rita. *American Smooth.* New York: Norton, 2004.

Falk, Marcia. *The Song of Songs: Love Poems from the Bible.* Illus. Barry Moser. New York: Harcourt Brace Jovanovich, 1977.

Ferlinghetti, Lawrence. *Coney Island of the Mind.* New York: New Directions, 1958.

———. *Ferlinghetti's Greatest Poems.* New York: New Directions, 2017.

———. *When I Look at Pictures.* Salt Lake City: Peregrine Smith Books, 1990.

Ghalib, Mirza. *The Lightning Should Have Fallen on Ghalib.* Trans. Robert Bly and Sunil Dutta. Hopewell, N.J.: Ecco Press, 1999.

Ghigna, Charles. *Tickle Day: Poems from Father Goose.* New York: Hyperion, 1994.

———. *Animal Tracks: Wild Poems to Read Aloud.* New York: Abrams, 2004.

Ginsberg, Allen. *Howl.* San Francisco: City Lights, 1959.

Gioia, Dana. *Interrogations at Noon.* Minneapolis: Graywolf, 2001.

Graves, Robert. *Collected Poems.* New York: Doubleday, 1961.

Harrison, Jim. *After Ikkyu and Other Poems.* Boston: Shambhala, 1996.

Herbert, George. *The Complete Works.* New York: Penguin Classics, 2015.

Hodges, Catherine Abbey. *Raft of Days.* Santa Barbara: Gunpowder Press, 2017.

Hopkins, Gerard Manley. *The Poems of Gerard Manley* Hopkins, Ed. W. H. Gardner and N. H. MacKenzie. London: Oxford Univ. Press, 1967.

Hudson, Robert. *Kiss the Earth When You Pray.* Illus. Mark Sheeres. Berkeley, Calif.: Apocryphile, 2016.

Hugo, Richard. *Selected Poems.* New York: Norton, 1979.

Issa, Kobayashi. *Cup-of-Tea Poems: Selected Haiku of Kobayashi Issa*. Trans. David Lanoue. Fremont, Calif.: Asian Humanities Press, 1991.

Jarman, Mark. *To the Green Man.* Louisville: Sarabande, 2004.

Johnson, Ronald. *Radi os.* Chicago: Flood Editions, 2005.

Kelly, Donika. *Bestiary.* Minneapolis: Gray Wolf Press, 2016.

Korreck, G. F. *Lowell Diary.* Grand Rapids, Mich.: Chapbook Press, 2015.

Leax, John. *Recluse Freedom.* Seattle, Wash.: WordFarm, 2012.

———. *Remembering Jesus: Sonnets and Songs.* Eugene, Ore.: Cascade, 2014.

———. *Tabloid News: Poems.* La Porte, Ind.: WordFarm, 2010.

Lee, David. *News from Down to the Café: New Poems.* Port Townsend, Wash.: Copper Canyon, 1999.

Lowell, Robert. *Life Studies: New Poems.* New York: Farrar, Straus and Cuday, 1959.

Mabry, John R. *Salvation of the True Rock: The Sufi Poetry of Najat Ozkaya.* Berkeley, Calif.: Apocryphile, 2011.

McEntyre, Marilyn Chandler. *Drawn to the Light: Poems on Rembrandt's Religious Paintings.* Grand Rapids, Mich.: Eerdmans, 2003.

———. *The Color of Light: Poems on Van Gogh's Late Paintings.* Grand Rapids, Mich.: Eerdmans, 2007.

———. *In Quiet Light: Poems on Vermeer's Women.* Grand Rapids, Mich.: Eerdmans, 2000.

Marquis, Don. *The Best of Archy and Mehitabel.* New York: Everyman Library/Knopf, 2011.

Matthews, Sebastian. *Beginner's Guide to a Head-On Collision.* Pasadena: Red Hen Press, 2017.

Merrill, James. *Nights and Days.* New York: Macmillan, 1966.

Merton, Thomas. *Cables to the Ace, or Familiar Liturgies of Misunderstanding.* New York: New Directions, 1968.

Moore, Daniel Abdal-Hayy. *The Blind Beekeeper.* Syracuse: Syracuse Univ. Press, 2001.

Neruda, Pablo. *The Essential Neruda: Selected Poems.* Ed. Mark Eisner. San Francisco: City Lights Books, 2004.

———. *Love Poems.* Trans. Donald D. Walsh. New York: New Directions, 2008.

———. *Odes to Common Things.* Trans. Ken Krabbenhoft. New York: Bulfinch, 1994.

———. *Odes to Opposites.* Trans. Ken Krabbenhoft. New York: Bulfinch, 1995.

———. *Twenty Love Poems and a Song of Despair.* Trans. W. S. Merwin. San Francisco: Chronicle Books, 1993.

Nye, Naomi Shihab. *19 Varieties of Gazelle: Poems of the Middle East.* New York: HarperCollins, 2002.

———. *Honeybee: Poems and Short Prose.* New York: Greenwillow, 2008.

———. *Words Under the Words: Selected Poems.* Portland: Far Corner, 1995.

Phipps, Brian. *Before the Burning Bush.* San Marcos, Calif.: Saint Katherine Press, 2018.

Plath, Sylvia. *Ariel.* New York: Harper & Row, 1965.

———. *The Colossus and Other Poems.* New York: Vintage, 1968.

Rich, Adrienne. *The Dream of a Common Language.* New York: Norton, 1978.

Rimbaud, Arthur. *Complete Works, Selected Letters.* Trans. Wallace Fowlie. Chicago: Univ. of Chicago Press, 1967.

Rossetti, Dante Gabriel. *Poems and Translations: 1850–1870.* London: Oxford Univ. Press, 1968.

Rumi, Jelaluddin. *One-Handed Basket Weaving: Poems on the Theme of Work.* Trans. Coleman Barks. Athens, Ga.: Maypop, 1993.

Ryan, Kay. *Erratic Facts.* New York: Grove Press, 2015.

Rylant, Cynthia. *God Went to Beauty School.* New York: HarperTeen, 2003.

Sandburg, Carl. *The Complete Poems of Carl Sandburg: Revised and Expanded Edition.* Ed. Archibald MacLeish. Orlando: Harcourt, 1970.

Sexton, Anne. *Live or Die.* Boston: Houghton Mifflin, 1966.

———. *The Awful Rowing Toward God.* Boston: Houghton Mifflin, 1975.

Shakespeare, William. *Shakespeare's Sonnets.* The Arden Shakespeare. Ed. Katherine Duncan-Jones. London: Methuen, 2010.

Sidman, Joyce. *What the Heart Knows: Chants, Charms, and Blessings.* Illus. Pamela Zagarenski. Boston: Houghton Mifflin Harcourt, 2013.

Smith, Stevie. *All the Poems.* New York: New Directions, 2016.

Smith, Tracy K. *Life on Mars: Poems.* Minneapolis: Graywolf, 2011.

Snyder, Gary. *Riprap and Cold Mountain Poems.* San Francisco: North Point, 1990.

———. *This Present Moment: New Poems.* Berkeley, Calif.: 2015.

———. *Turtle Island.* New York: New Directions, 1974.

Stevens, Wallace. *Collected Poetry and Prose.* New York: Library of America, 1997.

Tagore, Amitendranath, trans. *Moments of Rising Mist: A Collection of Sung Landscape Poetry.* New York: Grossman, 1973.

Thomas, Dylan. *The Poems of Dylan Thomas.* New York: New Directions, 2003.

Traherne, Thomas. *Poetry and Prose.* Ed. Denise Inge. London: Society for Promoting Christian Knowledge, 2002.

Turco, Lewis. *The Compleat Melancholick: Being a Sequence of Found, Composite, and Composed Poems, Based Largely upon Robert Burton's The Anatomy of Melancholy.* Marina Del Ray, Calif.: Beiler, 1985.

Vuong, Ocean. *Night Sky with Exit Wounds.* Port Townsend, Wash.: Copper Canyon Press, 2016.

Wangerin, Walter, Jr. *The Absolute, Relatively Inaccessible.*

Eugene, Ore.: Cascade, 2017.

Wantling, William. *The Awakening.* London: Rapp & Whiting, 1968.

Whitman, Walt. *Poetry and Prose.* New York: Library of America, 1982.

Wilbur, Richard. *New and Collected Poems.* New York: Harcourt Brace Jovanovich, 1988.

Williams, William Carlos. *Pictures from Brueghel and Other Poems.* New York: New Directions, 1962.

Wordsworth, William. *Selected Poems of William Wordsworth.* London: Oxford Univ. Press, 1975.

———, and Samuel Taylor Coleridge. *Lyrical Ballads.* New York: Routledge, 1991 [1798].

Yeats, W. B. *The Collected Poems of W. B. Yeats.* New York: Macmillan, 1956.

Yolen, Jane. *The Radiation Sonnets: For My Love, in Sickness and in Health.* Chapel Hill, N.C.: Algonquin, 2003.

To learn more about Robert Hudson's other books, or to order his chapbook called *Making a Poetry Chapbook,* or to read his "Curious Little Books" blog, go to roberthudsonbooks.com

Endnotes

1. Juan Ramón Jiménez, *The Complete Perfectionist: A Poetics of Work* (New York: Doubleday, 1997), 150.

A Note to the Reader

1. Thomas Merton, *Contemplative Prayer* (New York: Herder and Herder, 1969), 43.

Chapter 1

1. Pablo Neruda, *The Essential Neruda: Selected Poems*, ed. Mark Eisner (San Francisco: City Lights Books, 2004), vii.

2. William Wordsworth and Samuel Taylor Coleridge, "Preface," *Lyrical Ballads* (New York: Routledge, 1991), 307.

3. Gerard Manley Hopkins, "God's Grandeur," *The Poems of Gerard Manley Hopkins*, ed. W. H. Gardner and N. H. MacKenzie (London: Oxford Univ. Press, 1967), 66.

4. Genesis 23:4 KJV.

Chapter 2

1. Ralph Waldo Emerson, quoted in Edward Waldo Emerson, *Emerson in Concord: A Memoir* (Boston: Houghton Mifflin, 1889). 241.

2. Joan Acocella, "Prophet Motive: The Kahlil Gibran Phenomenon," *The New Yorker,* January 7, 2008.

3. I would guess that former US poet laureate Juan Felipe Herrera writes about at least half of those things in his collection *Notes on the Assemblage* (San Francisco: City Lights, 2015).

4. E. E. Cummings quoted in Richard S. Kennedy, *E. E. Cummings Revisited* (New York: Twayne, 1994), 8. Italics mine.

5. Randall Jarrell, "The Obscurity of the Poet," *Poetry and the Age* (London: Faber and Faber, 1996), 14.

6. Juan Ramón Jiménez, *The Complete Perfectionist: A Poetics of Work* (New York: Doubleday, 1997), 150.

7. Naomi Shihab Nye, *Words Under the Words: Selected Poems* (Portland: Far Corner, 1995). This is also the title to one of the poems in that book.

8. Saint Augustine, *On Christian Doctrine,* 18:28, from *The Nicene and Post-Nicene Fathers of the Christian Church,* Volume 2, ed. Philip Schaff (Grand Rapids, Mich.: Eerdmans, 1993), 544–45.

9. Saint Augustine, *Confessions,* 8:12, from *The Nicene and Post-Nicene Fathers of the Christian Church,* Volume 1, ed. Philip Schaff (Grand Rapids, Mich.: Eerdmans, 1993), 127.

Chapter 3

1. Jean Cocteau, in *The Ultimate Book of Quotations,* ed. Joseph Demakis (Charleston, S.C.: CreateSpace, 2012), 406.

2. This and all the Billy Collins quotes in this chapter are from Terri Gross, *Fresh Air,* NPR interview with Billy Collins (September 26, 2001): www.npr.org/2001/09/26/1130374/u-s-poet-laureate-billy-collins. The entire interview is moving and worth listening to.

3. Psalms 51:10; 57:1 KJV.

4. Thomas Merton, *Entering the Silence: Becoming a Monk and Writer* (New York: HarperCollins, 1996), 384.

5. Caedmon, "Caedmon's Hymn," *Old English Poetry*: http://www.english.illinois.edu/-people-/faculty/debaron/403/403%20old%20english/oe%20poems.html. We will look at Caedmon in more detail in chapter 8.

6. G. K. Chesterton, from "Variations on an Air," "Old King Cole," from *The Brand-X Anthology of Poetry: A Parody Anthology,* ed. William Zaranka (Cambridge, Mass.: Apple-Wood, 1981), 210.

7. Saint John of the Cross (1542–1591), *The Dark Night of the Soul*, chapter 16, section 12.

8. Anonymous Franciscan lay apostolate, quoted at *Quozio*, http://quozio.com/quote/9e88b766#!t=1025.

9. Psalm46:10.

10. Maurice Sendak, *Where the Wild Things Are* (New York: Harper & Row, 1963).

11. William Stafford, "The Center," *A Scripture of Leaves* (Elgin, Ill.: Brethren Press, 1989), 52.

12. William Stafford, *Writing the Australian Crawl* (Ann Arbor, Mich.: Univ. of Michigan Press, 1978), 152.

13. Wendell Berry, "X," *A Timbered Choir: The Sabbath Poems 1979–1997* (New York: Counterpoint, 1998), 149.

Chapter 4

1. Mirza Ghalib, "About My Poems," *The Lightning Should Have Fallen on Ghalib*, trans. Robert Bly and Sunil Dutta (Hopewell, N.J.: Ecco Press, 1999), 32.

2. George Mackay Brown, "The Poet," *Poems: New and Selected* (New York: Harcourt Brace Jovanovich, 1971), 79.

3. T. S. Eliot, *The Sacred Wood: Essays on Poetry and Criticism* (London: Methuen, 1920), 114.

4. Robert Hudson, "On Dying," *Kiss the Earth When You Pray* (Berkeley, Calif.: Apocryphile, 2016), 61.

Chapter 5

1. Lu Chi, *Wen Fu,* translated by Asano Karasu. Used by permission.

2. W. B. Yeats, "Lapis Lazuli," *The Collected Works of W. B. Yeats, Vol. 1, The Poems* (New York: Simon & Schuster, 1997), 301.

3. Percy Bysshe Shelley, in H. F. B. Brett-Smith, ed., *Peacock's Four Ages of Poetry; Shelley's Defence of Poetry; Browning's Essay on Shelley* (Boston: Houghton Mifflin, 1921), 56.

4. William Butler Yeats, *Letters to the New Island* (Cambridge, Mass.: Harvard Univ. Press, 1934), 43.

Chapter 6

1. Carl Sandburg, "Tentative (First Model) Definitions of Poetry, No. 37," *The Complete Poems of Carl Sandburg: Revised and Expanded Edition*, ed. Archibald MacLeish (Orlando: Harcourt, 1970), 319.

2. The poem is found in Helen Keller, *To Live, To Think, To Hope: Inspirational Quotes by Helen Keller*, ed. Matthew Gordon (CreateSpace, 2011), 170–71.

3. Helen Keller, from a letter to "My dear Mr. Hitz," *Selected Writings* (New York: New York Univ. Press, 2005), 11.

4. Richard Wilbur, "Love Calls Us to the Things of This World," *New and Collected Poems* (New York: Harcourt, Brace, Jovanovich, 1988), 233–34.

5. Matsuo Basho, "haiku," unpublished translation by Asano Karasu. Used with permission.

6. Samuel Taylor Coleridge, "Fears in Solitude: Written in April 1798 During the Alarm of an Invasion," *The Oxford Book of War Poetry*, ed. John Stallworthy (Oxford: Oxford Univ. Press, 1984), 72.

7. Samuel Taylor Coleridge, *Letters of Samuel Taylor Coleridge, Volume 1*, ed. Ernest Hartley Coleridge (London: Heinemann, 1895), 405–6. Italics in original.

8. Ernesto Cardenal, *To Live Is to Love* (New York: Herder and Herder, 1972), 46–47.

9. Psalm 139:13 KJV.

Chapter 7

1. Rachel Tzvia Back, "'A Species of Magic': The Role of Poetry in Protest and Truth-Telling (An Israeli Poet's Perspective)," *World Literature Today*, May–August 2014, https://www.worldliteraturetoday.org/2014/may/species-magic-role-poetry-protest-and-truth-telling-israeli-poets-perspective

2. William Blake, *Jerusalem*, 5:18–20.

Chapter 8

1. William Blake, "The Land of Dreams," *Blake: Complete Writings*, ed. Geoffrey Keynes (London: Oxford Univ. Press, 1972), 427.

2. From François Villon, "Le Petite Testament," translated by C. D. Matin.

3. Emily Dickinson, *Emily Dickinson's Poems—As She Preserved Them* (Cambridge, Mass.: Harvard Univ. Press, 2016), 270.

4. Rita Dove, "Chocolate," *American Smooth* (New York: Norton, 2004), 89.

5. Sir Philip Sidney, "The Defense of Poetry," *Miscellaneous Prose of Sir Philip Sidney*, eds. Katherine Duncan-Jones and Jan Van Dorsen (Oxford: Oxford Univ. Press, 1973), 78.

6. Percy Bysshe Shelley, in H. F. B. Brett-Smith, *Peacock's Four Ages of Poetry, Shelley's Defence of Poetry, Browning's Essay on Shelley* (Boston: Houghton Mifflin, 1921), 33.

7. Dylan Thomas, "In My Craft or Sullen Art," *The Poems of Dylan Thomas* (New York: New Directions, 2003), 227.

8. Arthur Rimbaud, "Lettre à Paul Demeny, 15 mai, 1871," trans. C. D. Matin.

9. Arthur Rimbaud, "Voyelles," trans. C. D. Matin.

10. Robert Hudson, "Reply to Rimbaud," *Mars Hill Review* 14 (winter 2000), 102. All of the rhymes in this sonnet were based on a, e, i, o, and u, in that order.

11. Keith M. Opdahl (1934–2013), who was professor of English at DePauw University,

12, Lawrence Ferlinghetti, *Poetry as Insurgent Art* (New York: New Directions, 2007), 39.

13. Scholars question the authorship of the hymn, just as they question the psalms of David. But the poem has an undeniable rugged beauty no matter who wrote it. What parts, if any, were actually written in a dream, we don't know. But it is a beautiful story.

14. Caedmon, "Caedmon's Hymn," *Old English Poetry*: http://www.english.illinois.edu/-people-/faculty/debaron/403/403%20old%20english/oe%20poems.html. Translated by Robert Hudson.

15. Coleridge tells this story in the preface to his volume *Cristabel, Kubla Khan, and the Pains of Sleep* (1816). It should be noted that scholars who have studied Coleridge's early drafts of "Kubla Kahn" doubt the veracity of his account. He seems to have been self-dramatizing to a great extent. Still, I like his story.

16. Robert Hudson, "On Growing Old," *Kiss the Earth When You Pray* (Berkeley, Calif.: Apocryphile Press), 60.

Chapter 9

1. Alice Walker, "Expect Nothing," *Anything We Love Can Be Saved* (New York: Ballantine, 1997), 90.

2. Hakuin Ekaku, *Wild Ivy: The Spiritual Autobiography of Zen Master Hakuin* (Boulder. Colo.: Shambhala, 1999), xxxvi.

3. Charles Baudelaire, "Les sept vieillards," *Fleurs du mal,* trans. C. D. Matin.

4. James Tate, *The Route as Briefed* (Ann Arbor, Mich.: Univ. of Michigan Press, 1999), 167.

5. Kobayashi Issa, "haiku," unpublished translation by Asano Karasu. Used with permission.

6. W. H. Davies, "All in June," *The Complete Poems of W. H. Davies* (Middletown, Conn.: Wesleyan Univ. Press, 1963), 502.

7. W. B. Yeats, "The Second Coming," *The Collected Poems of W. B. Yeats* (New York: Macmillan, 1956), 158.

8. Thomas Traherne, "Wonder," *The Works of Thomas Traherne*, Vol. VI, ed. Jan Ross (Suffolk: D. S. Brewer, 2014), 90.

9. William Wordsworth, "Ode [Intimations of Immortality]," *The New Oxford Book of Romantic Period Verse*, ed. Jerome J. McGann (Oxford: Oxford Univ. Press, 1993), 269.

10. Robert Graves, *Oxford Addresses on Poetry* (London: Cassell, 1961), 111.

Chapter 10

1. Rosemarie Waldrop quoted in "All My Poems Are Love Poems: When Two Poets Fall in Love," *poets.org*, February 9, 2007, https://www.poets.org/poetsorg/text/all-my-poems-are-love-poems-when-two-poets-fall-love. The full quote is "All my poems are really love poems for Keith" (her husband).

2. Helen Vendler, *The Art of Shakespeare's Sonnets* (Cambridge, Mass.: Belknap, 1997), 206.

3. Gregory Corso, "Marriage," *The Happy Birthday of Death* (New York: New Directions, 1960), 32.

4. Andrew Marvell, "To His Coy Mistress," *The Complete Poems* (New York: St. Martin's, 1974), 51.

5. John Keats, "Bright Star," *The Complete Poems* (London: Penguin, 1988), 452.

6. Robert Graves, "Counting the Beats," *Collected Poems* (New York: Doubleday, 1961), 265.

7. Dylan Thomas, "You Are the Ruler of the Realm of Flesh," *The Poems of Dylan Thomas* (New York: New Directions, 2003), 63.

8. Thomas Hardy, "The Shadow on the Stone," *The Complete Poems* (New York: Macmillan, 1982), 530.

9. Bruce Springsteen, "Wreck on the Highway," *The River* (Columbia, 1980), side 4, track 4.

10. Elizabeth Barrett Browning, Sonnet 43 from *Sonnets from the Portuguese*, in W. Peacock, ed., *English Verse: Volume IV: From Sir Walter Scott to Elizabeth Barrett Browning* (London: Oxford Univ. Press, 1971), 596.

Chapter 11

1. John Keats, "Where be ye going, you Devon maid?" *The Complete Poems* (London: Penguin, 1988), 234.

2. Schuler Books of Grand Rapids, Michigan.

3. Tseng Kung, "Tower at Kan-lu Monastery," *Moments of Rising Mist: A Collection of Sung Landscape Poetry*, trans Amitendranath Tagore (New York: Grossman, 1973), 123.

Chapter 12

1. W. H. Auden, *The Dyer's Hand and Other Essays* (New York: Random House, 1962), 22.

2. Both quotes are reported by others and are not found in the writings of Chesterton and Frost themselves. As mentioned, they are frequently quoted in books on poetry writing, but I have not tracked down the original sources, though some sources quote Frost as having said, "... with the net down."

3. W. H. Auden, *The Dyer's Hand and Other Essays* (New York: Random House, 1962), 22.

4. Dylan Thomas, *The Caedmon Collection* 11 CDs (New York: Caedmon/HarperAudio, 2002), discs 5–7.

5. T. S. Eliot, "Dante," *Selected Essays 1917–1932* (New York: Harcourt, Brace and Company, 1932), 200.

6. Dante Alighieri, *The Divine Comedy of Dante Alighieri: Volume 1: Inferno*, trans. Robert M. Durling (Oxford: Oxford Univ. Press, 1996), 26.

7. The epigram by Coleridge, which is usually dated 1802, and the anecdote about his grandmother are in: eds. Theodore Bonnet and Edward F. O'Day, "A Few Epigrams," *The Lantern*, vol. 2, no. 2 (May 1916), 65.

8. Aristotle, *Aristotle's Art of Poetry*, ed. W. Hamilton Fyfe (London: Oxford Univ. Press, 1967), 4.

9. Arthur Clutton-Brock, *William Morris: His Work and Influence* (London: Williams & Norgate, 1914), 40.

10. I should insert that Frost was a writer of quite hard-hitting poems, even many that didn't rhyme, like his famous "Out, Out—," which is one of the most powerful blank verse poems in modern English.

11. Learn more about Waller's work at Stephen J. Waller, "Rock Art Acoustics," https://sites.google.com/site/rockartacoustics/.

12. John Keats, "On the Grasshopper and the Cricket," *Poetical Works* (London: Oxford Univ. Press, 1972), 40.

13. One of the best online references is the Poetry Foundation's *Glossary of Poetic Terms*, https://www.poetryfoundation.org/learn/glossary-terms.

Chapter 13

1. Jack Kerouac, attributed; no known source.

2. Dylan Thomas, *The Collected Letters of Dylan Thomas*, ed. Paul Ferris (New York: Macmillan, 1986), 487. Thomas most likely read Rimbaud in translation.

3. Walt Whitman, "Song of Myself," *Poetry and Prose* (New York: Library of America, 1982), 204–5.

4. T. S. Eliot, "The Love Song of J. Alfred Prufrock," *The Complete Poems and Plays of T. S. Eliot* (London: Faber and Faber, 1969), 13–14.

5. Emily Dickinson, "A narrow Fellow in the Grass," *Emily Dickinson's Poems as She Preserved Them*, ed. Cristanne Miller (Cambridge, Mass.: Belknap, 2016), 490.

6. Quoted in a 1975 article by Hannah Arendt, "Remembering Wystan H. Auden," *Thinking Without a Banister: Essays in Understanding, 1953–1975* (New York: Random House, 2018), 527.

7. Quoted in Robert Graves, *The White Goddess: A Historical Grammar of Poetic Myth* (New York: Farrar, Straus & Giroux, 2013), 16.

Chapter 14

1. Jean-Charles Nault, *The Noonday Devil: Acedia, the Unnamed Evil of Our Times* (San Francisco: Ignatius, 2015), 134.

2. Gerard Manley Hopkins, "Thou art indeed just, Lord, if I contend," *The Poems of Gerard Manley Hopkins* (London: Oxford Univ. Press, 1967), 106–7. This is not to say that all was well with Hopkins after this time. This rush of great poems, some of which Hopkins referred to as his "terrible sonnets," were written at a time of great loneliness and disappointment. He died three months after completing this poem.

3. Wallace Stevens, *The Letters of Wallace Stevens*, ed. Holly Stevens (Berkeley, Calif.: Univ. of California Press, 1996), 115. This letter is dated January 6, 1909.

4. John Keats, from a March 1819 letter, *Selected Letters of John Keats*, ed. Grant F. Scott (Cambridge, Mass.: Harvard Univ. Press, 2002), 262–63.

5. Franz Kafka, *Diaries 1914–1923* (New York: Schocken, 1949), 107, 111, 113–14, 116.

6. Helen Darbishire, ed. *Journals of Dorothy Wordsworth* (London: Oxford Univ. Press, 1958), 105, 109, 110–12, 114–15, 138–39.

7. Jean-Charles Nault, *The Noonday Devil: Acedia, the Unnamed Evil of Our Times* (San Francisco: Ignatius, 2015), 135.

8. Layli Long Soldier, "Layli Long Soldier on Poetry as Prayer," *The Creative Independent* (February 27, 2017), https://thecreativeindependent.com/people/layli-long-soldier-on-poetry-as-prayer/.

9. Robert Hudson, "On Prayer 3," *Kiss the Earth When You Pray* (Berkeley, Calif.: Apocryphile, 2016), 24.

10. Joost van den Vondel, *Lucifer*, act 2. The line means, roughly, "It is better to be the first prince in a lower court than in the blessed light to be a subordinate or even lower." Vondel's Lucifer was one of Milton's sources for *Paradise Lost*, and this line inspired Milton's famous line "Better to reign in Hell, than serve in Heaven" (1:263).

Chapter 15

1. Gene Beley, *Ray Bradbury: Uncensored!: The Unauthorized Biography* (Lincoln, Neb.: iUniverse, 2006), 183.

2. Mac Davis, "Stop and Smell the Roses," written by Mac Davis and Doc Severinsen (Columbia, 1974), 45rpm vinyl recording. The quote originated with golf great Walter Hagen who recommended that people "stop and smell the flowers along the way."

3. Ilya Tolstoy, *Reminiscences of Leo Tolstoy*, trans. George Calderon (New York: Century, 1914), 111.

4. W. B. Yeats, "Long-legged Fly," *The Collected Works of W. B. Yeats, Vol. 1, The Poems* (New York: Simon & Schuster, 1997), 347.

5. Masaoka Shiki, "haiku," unpublished translation by Asano Karasu. Used by permission.

6. Thomas Merton, *Contemplative Prayer* (New York: Herder and Herder, 1969), 118.

7. Ryokan Taigu, "Why do people tell me my poems are poems?" unpublished translation by Asano Karasu. Used with permission.

8. Walter Gieseking and Karl Leimer, *Piano Technique* (New York: Dover, 1972).

Chapter 16

1. Frederick William Robertson, *Life, Letters, Lectures, and Addresses* (New York: Harper and Brothers, 1978), 786. In this quote, Robertson, a popular Victorian preacher, was criticizing the poetry of Alexander Pope as being too cerebral.

2. Aristotle, "Problems Connected with Thought, Intelligence, and Wisdom," quoted in Jennifer Radden, ed., *The Nature of Melancholy: From Aristotle to Kristeva* (Oxford: Oxford Univ. Press, 2000), 57.

3. Robert Burton, *Anatomy of Melancholy* (Oxford: Benediction Classics, 2017 [1621]), 57. He was quoting an ancient commentator on Virgil.

4. Quoted in Eric Maisel, *The Van Gogh Blues: The Creative Person's Path through Depression* (Novato, Calif.: New World Library, 2002), 4.

5. Alice W. Flaherty, *The Midnight Disease: The Drive to Write: Writer's Block, and the Creative Brain* (Boston: Houghton Mifflin, 2004), 33.

6. Kobayashi Issa, "haiku," unpublished translation by Asano Karasu.

7. Makoto Ueda, Matsuo Basho: *The Master Haiku Poet* (New York: Kodansha, 1982), 176.

Chapter 17

1. Phyllis McGinley, interviewed in Harvey Breit, *The Writer Observed* (Cleveland: World Publishing, 1956), 212.

2. Robert Shelton, *No Direction Home: The Life and Music of Bob Dylan* (Milwaukee: Backbeat Books, 2011), 35.

3. William Blake, "Annotations to Boyd's Dante," *Complete Writings* (London: Oxford Univ. Press, 1972), 412.

4. John Leax, *Grace Is Where I Live: The Landscape of Faith and Writing* (La Porte, Ind.: WordFarm, 2004), 29.

5. Quoted in Jan Blodgett, *Protestant Evangelical Culture and Contemporary Society* (Westport, Conn.: Greenwood, 1997), 33.

Chapter 18

1. Madeleine L'Engle, *Walking on Water: Reflections on Faith and Art* (New York: Random House, 2016), 183.

Chapter 19

1. Judson Jerome, *The Poet and the Poem* (Cincinnati: Writer's Digest Books, 1979), 13.

Chapter 20

1. T. S. Eliot, *The Use of Poetry and the Use of Criticism: Studies in the Relation of Criticism to Poetry in England* (London: Faber & Faber, 1964), 154.

2. Robert Hudson, "On Gratitude," *Kiss the Earth When You Pray* (Berkeley, Calif.: Apocryphile, 2016), 19.

Chapter 21

1. Robert Graves and Spike Milligan, *Dear Robert, Dear Spike: The Graves-Milligan Correspondence* (Phoenix Mill, Gloucestershire: Sutton, 1991), xx.

2. John Kennedy Toole, *A Confederacy of Dunces* (New York: Grove, 1980), 55.

3. M. Scott Peck, *The Road Less Traveled: A New Psychology of Love, Traditional Values, and Spiritual Growth* (New York: Touchstone, 2003).

4. Don Marquis, from one of his *Sun Dial* columns, quoted

in Edward Anthony, *O Rare Don Marquis: A Biography* (New York: Doubleday, 1962), 146.

Epilogue

1. Leonard Cohen, *The Favorite Game* (Toronto: McClelland & Stewart, 1994), 170.

2. Ray Bradbury, *Zen and the Art of Writing* (Santa Barbara: Capra, 1973), 29.

3. This story is related in a poem by Martín Espada, "The Soldiers in the Garden," *The Estate of Poetry* (New York: Norton, 2006), 12–13.

4. Quoted in Barry Miles, *Allen Ginsberg: A Biography* (New York: HarperPerennial, 1990), 520.

5. Matthew Arnold, "The Study of Poetry, Essays in Criticism (New York: A. L. Burt, 1900), 281.

6. 1 Peter 2:11 KJV.

Made in the USA
Middletown, DE
16 February 2019